The secrets of success at work

10 steps to accelerating your career

Second edition

Richard Hall

Prentice Hall
Business
is an imprint of

Harlow, England • London • New York • Boston • San Francisco • Toronto
Sydney • Tokyo • Singapore • Hong Kong • Seoul • Taipei • New Delhi
Cape Town • Madrid • Mexico City • Amsterdam • Munich • Paris • Milan

PEARSON EDUCATION LIMITED

Edinburgh Gate
Harlow CM20 2JE
Tel: +44 (0)1279 623623
Fax: +44 (0)1279 431059
Website: www.pearsoned.co.uk

First published in Great Britain in 2008
Second edition published 2011

ISBN: 978-0-273-74294-4

British Library Cataloguing-in-Publication Data
A catalogue record for this book is available from the British Library

Library of Congress Cataloging-in-Publication Data
Hall, Richard, 1944-
     The secrets of success at work : 10 steps to accelerating your career / Richard Hall. -- 2nd ed.
        p. cm.
     ISBN 978-0-273-74294-4 (pbk.)
  1. Success in business. 2. Interpersonal communication. 3. Success--Psychological aspects. 4. Career development. I. Title.
   HF5386.H2357 2011
   650.1--dc22
                                                      2010030275

10 9 8 7 6 5 4 3 2 1
14 13 12 11 10

Text design by Sue Lamble
Cartoons © Bill Piggins
Typeset in 10 pt Iowan Old Style by 30
Printed in Great Britain by Henry Ling Ltd, at the Dorset Press, Dorchester, Dorset.

Warning!

We live in dangerous times.

The world is in turmoil.

Anyone who says it is easy to succeed is a liar – it's never been harder.

But in this epic adventure of confusion I find hope and opportunity for the brave, fleet-footed and innovative.

Never have the rewards for 'going for it' been so good if you have good plans, great product, a strong brand, self belief plus the following:

◆ luck

◆ skill

◆ energy

◆ tenacity

The real secret of success at work lies in your saying 'I can' with conviction and confidence.

Well it worked for Obama ...

Read on, enjoy and good luck.

Contents

Foreword

THINK OF THIS as being a book-sized career manual.

When it comes to planning our lives and our careers and then trying to make the plan come true, most of us live in a fog of confusion. Few have a destination in mind. Even fewer have a route map.

We have a vague sense about getting on and doing well but few of us are sure exactly why and spend periods of our lives slightly or very discontented.

The word 'career' itself is a bit strange.

It sounds, surprisingly, much more exciting: full of images of surging speed, racing, shooting stars, momentum and, perhaps surprisingly, more of a sprint than a marathon.

Hawks and racehorses seem generally to know where they are going and they do it with style, speed and focus. So let's take that need for speed as the first thing to tackle.

Not rocket science you say – and you are right. It's much more complex. Any fool can build a rocket. Very few can build careers that give them what they deserve, let alone a lot more.

Have a destination, have a map, have a plan and recognise – pragmatically – that doing well in your career and being good at

it's not always the cleverest who do best

doing your job are not necessarily going to be the same thing. It's like exams – it's not always the cleverest who do best.

So here are ten strategies for maximising your chances of doing well or much better than you'd hoped. They are shameless crutches on which to lean and with which to leverage your talents so you look as good as possible. It's about marketing yourself so you achieve the best you can.

I want you to win even when you shouldn't; get promoted; get an eye-watering salary increase when you were worried about being fired.

But most of all I want you to have fun.

Even in the toughest times we should aim to enjoy life.

As Jerry of Ben & Jerry fame (and very considerable ice cream wealth) reflected:

'If you don't enjoy it why do it?'

This book tells you how to win and enjoy yourself doing it.

Richard Hall
www.richardhall.biz
richard@hallogram.freeserve.co.uk
http://marketing-creativity-leadership.blogspot.com/

Introduction

How to find your own 'WOW' factor (and then how to develop it)

YOUR WOW FACTOR IS THAT THING which everyone has, although many people keep it very well hidden, and which if nourished or encouraged would mark them out from the throng. Winston Churchill was hopeless academically, the incredibly rich Felix Dennis – entrepreneur and author – was allegedly worse, J.K. Rowling was unpublished until she thought of *Harry Potter* and the rest is, well, the rest is magic.

They all had or have WOW factors that they identified and developed.

But what is WOW? It stands for 'Walk on Water'. It's that moment 'when one's wonderful' – when you've made a good speech or you're revelling in your manager's praise.

it's a moment of sheer infallibility

It's a moment of sheer infallibility, when nothing is impossible, when you want them all to 'bring it on'.

(And it also stands for 'Wow!' – that noise you make when you are incredibly impressed by something or someone. Amazement and awe in just three letters.)

Everyone has moments in their life when they do something that turns on a light in their head and when they become reborn in some intriguing way. It's that moment when you – and the outside world – look on yourself with new eyes and see new talent. It is, in short, a career-defining moment.

It's like falling in love. But falling in love with what you do, in the office.

Making the magic of WOW happen

By believing you can

You don't hope for the best, you don't pray for it, you visualise yourself doing it. The next time someone says, 'Can you do something?' say 'Yes', and then work out how you are going to get it done.

By practice

Congratulations. You've taken my advice. You're down to speak at an annual company conference and you're really not that skilled at public speaking. So that's another fine mess I've got you into. Will you sink like a stone or walk on water? First of all believe in yourself, secondly set aside lots of time to work on the presentation, thirdly get some one-to-one presentation coaching (which the company will pay for because it's actually in its interest to do so). But most of all practise, practise, practise.

By working with a sponsor

Someone senior you like and trust who will help you in constructing your presentation and make the idea of 'WOW' come to life. Someone who will mentor you. They themselves probably 'wing' it a bit now, but in you they'll see the energy, hope and nervousness of a younger them.

Walking on water is what happens when you believe in yourself, work at it, share ideas and listen to experts.

Examples of WOW moments

Re-launching yourself

The deliberate attempt to change the way you are perceived.

'She was a very attractive woman. She was loved and admired by a lot of people but they'd got comfortable with her. She was a little in the "good old ..." category. The sort of person you could always rely on. Not so much WOW as MOM. One day to everyone's surprise she went blonde. Very blonde. And everyone took notice. Someone said, "It was like the sun coming out. I looked at her afresh instead of taking her for granted, and I said – WOW."'

Becoming a challenger, a questioner and an advocate

It's called discovering your critical faculty.

'He was promoted in his first job. That felt terrific; he felt he deserved it but was none the less pleased. And then his critical faculty kicked in – Why this? How that? Why not try...? – that sparked off an amazing energy surge and he became a somewhat antagonistic, highly competitive and impatient brand manager who became a question machine in a hurry. "I knew I could walk on water because I knew my stuff, I knew intuitively how to do magic and how to connect with the consumer – I just knew. I also knew I could and would win." Under his stewardship a number 2 or 3 going – nowhere brand became brand leader in months.' WOW.

Being asked to join the club of the accomplished

A WOW moment for many is being accepted by your peers.

A potter friend of mine was recently invited to display her 'art' with the Sussex Guild, a fairly choosy group of extraordinary craftspeople, at its show at Michelham Priory, Upper Dicker in Sussex. Invited along for support, I was sceptical at first until I realised I was in the presence of vast talent and possibly, from time to time, pure genius; people who loved what they did and lived for it. My potter friend was aglow with the pride of acceptance by her peers. WOW.

Focusing on what you want to do

We only have one life. WOW.

I read about a guy who had a horrendous accident on a ski lift that collapsed, crushing him and leaving him clawing his way back to safety with his one good hand. Certain death behind him, an agonising climb in front. He survived and after a long convalescence resigned from an important, well paid job and started his own business. His lesson? We only have one life. WOW.

Keeping faith with your vision and never giving up

Henry Heinz of blessed baked bean fame had a vision – literally. He believed that by making a great-looking, pure product and putting it in transparent jars the potential consumer could see how good it was. His business failed a couple of times before it roared into life. He put on his bowler hat, left America and made his way to London, to Fortnum & Mason. The buyer accepted all six products Henry showed him – and Heinz was made. This was a triumph of vision over initial reverses; a stubborn determination to focus on success. WOW.

You can't believe you can walk on water until you have that sudden moment of self-belief, then you take a first step and WOW it happens, it suddenly happens.

So you've walked on water – once or twice. How do you develop it? How do you keep it up?

Learning to develop that walk-on-water walk

Once you've tasted that unbeatable feeling it'll be hard to forget it, or not want to repeat it again and again. Here's how you do that.

Remember the feeling of that first breakthrough moment

What triggered it? Go through a pre-flight check before you try to recreate it so all the conditions and expectations are the same. It's what any pilot or good presenter does. It's what any 'water-walker' always does.

Build your self-confidence

You do this through really knowing your stuff. You won't walk on water if your knowledge is leaky. Always be

be prepared to withstand any amount of challenge or rebuttal

prepared, know your story, know the facts. And be prepared to withstand any amount of challenge or rebuttal.

Always be ready to present your case

Don't be caught on the hop. Be ready to stand up and sock it to them. More walk-on-water moments are achieved by a good public performance than anything else. The more practised you are as a presenter the more effective your walking will be.

Deserve praise and make sure you get it

Without feedback you have no radar system. What's more the most apparently self-confident person still needs to be told they have done well, that they have been a star and, indeed even, that they have really done brilliantly. Work with people who always give you honest feedback. But work with people who make you feel good about yourself so their feedback, even if critical, also focuses on the effective bits of your performance.

Building that walking-on-water feeling so it becomes second nature

Once that sense of 'I can really do this and do it well' hits you, once you know you can actually walk on water, you'll want to do it again and again:

◆ You build on it by practice, by rehearsing more and in a more focused way than anyone else in your company.

◆ You build on it by trying to see things from other points of view.

◆ You build on it by hanging on to the memory or vision of what it actually feels like to win.

◆ You build on it by trying to love what you do; by exuding a real sense of exuberance about what you do and how you do it.

◆ You really build on it by teaching others how to achieve it too. The best way of reinforcing your learning is by teaching others how to do as well or better than you.

Visualise that walk-on-water moment and you're halfway towards making it a norm as opposed to an exception.

Retaining that WOW feeling

Retaining the WOW feeling needs good and caring management from those above you but, for your part, you need to make those around you feel good about you and believe that they are working with a winner. Confidence is fragile – don't break it by careless indifference. Don't take it for granted because that 'winning feeling' is uniquely special – ask anyone in sport who's been on a roll.

keep the magic going as long as possible

I believe it's the role of all leaders to get their people to feel as though they can walk on water, to create an exclusive WOW club that everyone wants to join. It's also their role to keep the magic going for as long as possible.

But we live in strange times and nothing is certain for-ever. The one thing we all have to be (and it's essential we retain this) is confident that we will always do our best, and do it calmly and quickly.

How do you measure WOW?

Ask an actor and they'll probably answer, 'By the applause level.' It's a cross between your own self-awareness and a powerful sense of empathy you create with whoever your audience is – your boss, your board, your peers, your staff, your customers.

As I write this book a young man is learning to juggle outside our house on the green. Yesterday he was really pretty awful and kept on dropping the third skittle. He'd then do it with two and include some fancy moves as well. But juggling with two is easy isn't it?

Today, after hours of practice, I saw a huge improvement in his performance. He was juggling with three skittles for longer and then with a bottle and two cups. As often as he dropped one he regrouped and tried again.

I suspect his WOW moment will come next week if he carries on like this.

Donald Bradman, the cricketer and the world's best ever batsman, practised with a cricket stump and a golf ball thrown against a barn wall. All great golfers practise virtually non-stop. For them it is their life. WOW equals 'work-oh-work'. The harder you work and the more you try the better you will do.

WOW happens when you focus on whatever things you are best at or at which you could be exceptional if you tried hard enough.

Jack Welch, whom most would agree was the greatest CEO of our generation, said:

Determine your own destiny or someone else will.

Things to think about

◆ *You create your WOW moment by having that liberating feeling of self-determination and then really going for it.*

◆ *So get yourself in the best 'I can really do it' mindset and you too may have that 'walk-on-water' feeling.*

◆ *Create stimulus around yourself.*

◆ *If you feel good, you'll probably be good.*

◆ *Discovering, building on and retaining WOW is a mind thing which then leads to a successful performance thing which then leads on to an employer appreciation thing and it is one you can easily achieve if you think hard and positively enough about it.*

◆ *You also have to be prepared to take risks – to put yourself on stage doing a presentation or in a meeting arguing a case with the risk of failure.*

Go for it. See how many WOW moments you can have this week.

1

Look in the mirror. That's the real you … say hallo and be amazed

Why knowing yourself well is a powerful secret weapon.

WHILST ALL THE EXPERTS, FROM MOTIVATIONAL WRITERS to the most inspirational gurus, will tell you that achievement of just about anything is in your grasp, that all you have to do is want it enough, no-one explains that you have to understand what you are working with. So you could be a concert pianist, county cricketer, writer of business books. It's easy peasy, they suggest. Just dream it and do it.

Hmmmm!!!! That's what I say. Let's not underestimate this rise to glory.

And without the absolute certainty of who you are, what you are, your pluses and minuses, and your hopes and fears, you really aren't going to get very far.

But how well do you know yourself already?

On the face of it this seems an absurd question to ask. You ought to know yourself very well since you've been your most constant companion all your life. But you've probably paid little attention to yourself, to how others see you and how you see yourself.

As so often, we miss the most obvious things in life. We take ourselves for granted. We miss what's sitting in front of us. Our unfulfilled talent – our WOW factor — hiding under that ton of modesty.

This failure to be a 'me-expert' leads to some very odd decisions that we make in life. Like quite simply ending up in the wrong job for which we are wildly unsuited. Like waking up one morning and finding we have married the wrong person. Or, worse still, like waking up one morning, alone.

How self-knowledge can change your behaviour

This happened a very, very long time ago and I am not particularly proud of it. Three of us, after a Japanese meal with a lot of sake, went to a Soho strip club. The entrance fee was 10 shillings (50p in today's money).

> Seedy Soho. We went down a dirty narrow staircase. Cobwebs drifted across our faces. We heard ... nothing. Pushing open a filthy curtain we found ourselves in a large and untidy storeroom. My companions were uneasy, the more so when two large Mediterranean-looking guys appeared, aggressively telling

us to 'push off'. Yes, we had been conned. My companions legged it. Now whether it was the sake or a sense of injustice that left me rooted to the spot I can't be sure. I decided to reason with them. In fury they rushed at me with baseball bats, looking very menacing. 'Look, this is silly, you are intelligent chaps. Let me explain why I am unhappy.' My would-be assailants looked a little puzzled. 'Push off,' one said quietly, 'I'm not intelligent.' 'Of course you are,' I told him. 'I can see intelligence in your face.' 'What about me?' asked his colleague rather grumpily. I assured them they were both intelligent, very intelligent and that their behaviour was strange because it was at odds with this. They agreed with the analysis and led us all (my colleagues still waiting outside for me to emerge) to a proper strip joint further down Dean Street where strippers glorying under the names Patricia Bronte, Charlotte Eliot and Matilda Austen did their stuff. 'Sorry for the misunderstanding,' said my swarthy bouncers as they led us in. 'No, thank you. It's been a pleasure meeting you,' I said – and it had been. They even looked intelligent as they said goodbye and strode off into the night.

This is a story about them, not me. It was their confrontation with something that had been sublimated that resonated so powerfully in their brains. They were quite intelligent – they'd forgotten that's all. And when reminded they behaved gently and intelligently. Tell someone they are 'a fool' by the same token and see their behaviour worsen.

Getting to know you, getting to know all about you

self-knowledge is the single most powerful tool

Unless we work at knowing who we really are and what we could really do, we are unlikely to head in the right direction. But if we do work ourselves out and can say with confidence 'this is the real me' then we are in great shape to create a new and upward-looking career. Self-knowledge is the single most powerful tool for achieving the ideal job and career path that is right for you, not for that image of yourself that you'd like to have.

In simple terms, knowing the raw materials you've got to work with in 'making it happen' for your career is the starting point. Everything else is fantasy.

So you have to start by forensically testing who and what you are, and who you could be and who you are unlikely to be (however much you might want to be that ideal).

But a word of caution. This isn't easy. It needs you to work hard, dispassionately and with brutal honesty. It might even prove a little uncomfortable. Knowledge, as Adam and Eve discovered, comes at a cost.

Working out your strengths and weaknesses

Unless we bother to ask ourselves some really simple and important questions about where our talents and our passions at work lie, we'll miss out on the most basic and most useful self-analysis.

John Scott, a leading HR guy who heads HR at PWC in the Middle East, said:

Get someone to do something they really enjoy and you'll be looking at a successful person.

He then added, being a big, corporate HR guy, (actually he's not overly corporate in the worst sense of that word) that it maybe wasn't quite that simple.

Well it actually is that simple. Try this self-administered test and see how unfair previous appraisals have been.

In each quadrant of the chart you'll be seeing things you are good at or not so good at, and dislike or enjoy doing.

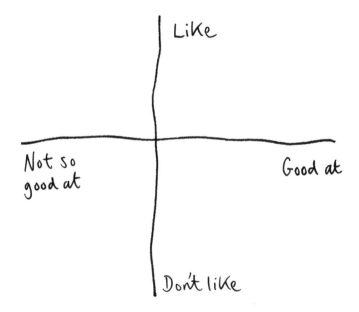

And here's the list of things I want you to put in the appropriate quadrant:

1 Data and maths

2 Writing reports

3 Working alone

4 Presenting

5 Coaching people

6 Criticising people

7 Praising people

8 Making things happen

9 Being creative

10 Delegating tasks

11 Leading people

12 Getting up to go to work on Mondays

13 Dealing with a crisis

14 Being tidy and well organised

15 Travelling

16 Having to work late or over the weekend

17 Being off-site

18 Selling

When you've done this exercise get two close colleagues and friends to give their view of you by doing the exercise as if in your shoes.

Be excited by the discoveries you make because they will give you a much more precise fix on the talent base, real and perceived, that you have to work with.

Apart from anything else you now have plenty of positive stuff to think about. Stuff that can inspire you to try harder; stuff that can help you make it really happen, happen fast and happen explosively; stuff that confirms hidden views about yourself like, 'I hate spreadsheets and I know Lucy is great at them'.

You now have a pretty good sense of the turbocharged vehicle – whoa! It's not turbocharged yet... but carry on reading – that will take you on your route map to your destination in life.

Creating the right first impressions

Assuming we have got a pretty good handle on our own self-analysis, most of our lives we need to do justice to ourselves and never more importantly than when meeting people for the first time.

We all know that it takes just a few minutes to decide if the person in front of you has an appealing personality and story to tell. That's why speed dating is so popular. That's why Malcolm Gladwell's book *Blink* resonates so powerfully. (It argues that very often snap judgements can be more effective than a cautious decision.) So play to that and make sure you always pass the 'snap judgement' test. Avoid the couldn't-care-less, take-me-as-you-find-me trait that can be so off-putting.

make sure you always pass the 'snap judgement' test

Kenneth Clark, MP and one-time contender for Conservative Party leadership, was one who simply didn't care how he looked. The trouble was he seemed incredibly scruffy. A brilliant mind and a powerful personality spoiled by an egg-splattered tie and scuffed suede shoes. First impressions are very important and the first impression we give is what we see in the mirror.

So the first piece of advice on this mission to improve our self-knowledge is to buy a full-length mirror and spend a long time looking at and thinking about ourselves. This is the raw material with which we have to work.

Narcissistic? Not really. It just helps you focus and maybe realise how to be a better actor. It might guide you to reflect on how to learn to be still as well as how to be engagingly energetic. How, in other words, to work with what you've got.

Knowing how others see us: taking a 360-degree view

Knowing yourself is terrific but knowing how you are perceived by others really takes you to another place. A position of greater power than you may ever have had before – a position from which to market yourself as opposed to just being yourself. And deep at the centre of this book is a belief we can make more of what we've got so as to please those we want to please if, that is, we know what we've got to work with in the first place.

How's your Scottish? No, mine's not that good either so I've translated what follows into simple English. Read Robert Burns the Scottish poet and be in the presence of wisdom:

Oh would some power the gift be given us

To see ourselves as others see us

It would from many a blunder free us
And foolish notion.

Burns describes this potential power as ego-reducing and risk- and mistake-averting. We'll talk about egos in a minute but here's a way of unleashing that power.

Divide a circle into six segments, containing those people closest to you, and work really hard on how you think the people in each of those segments regard you – your strengths and weaknesses – and how they are likely to be helpful to you. (See over the page for an example.)

If you find this hard to do, that will in itself have taught you something of value. And if you can't really do it at all (which I doubt) then do you have problems? Yes, you really do.

About losing your ego

There's a good ego – self-confident, self-esteem, happy, bravado ego. A well-balanced person ego. And there's a plaster-over and fill-in-the-character-cracks superiority complex covering up an inferiority complex sort of ego. In other words we are in Jekyll and Hyde territory.

Keep your confidence but lose that need to feed your self-glorification – and do it now. That may temporarily put an end to any thought of your becoming CEO but you may benefit from that.

I have seen many people with an ego bigger than their talent bent on a career of self-mortification by being seen as the worst of all mixes – arrogant and mediocre.

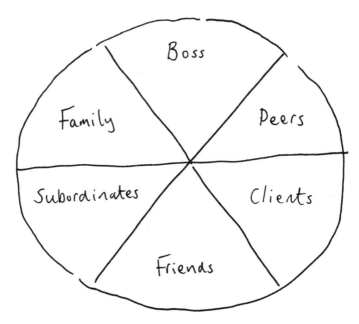

What do those close to you
really think of you?

You've got to accentuate the positive …

These lyrics by the American songwriter Johnny Mercer
should be carved on everyone's 'to do' list:

You've got to accentuate the positive

Eliminate the negative

Latch on to the affirmative

And don't mess with Mr In-between.

You've got to spread joy up to the maximum

Bring gloom down to the minimum

Otherwise pandemonium

Is liable to walk upon the scene.

Why I like this so much (although I'd be cautious about being too evangelical a spreader of joy as it can be a touch irritating if it's overdone) is that it squarely focuses on the key thing anyone seeking career success must have – a positive frame of mind.

But you can't go about accentuating, eliminating and latching on to, if you haven't got a pretty firm grasp of your personal assets. So let's carry on seeing how to refine that.

What is your bottom line?

There's a story about George Bernard Shaw, the great literary figure, intellectual and playwright of the first half of the 1900s. He sat next to a lady at a supper party and popped the question:

GBS: *'Would you sleep with me for a million pounds?'*

Lady: *'Oh Mr Shaw of course I would – you are such a wag.'*

GBS: *'Madam would you sleep with me for a pound?'*

Lady (in outrage): *'Mr Shaw what do you take me for?'*

GBS: *'We've already established what you are madam. Now we are merely haggling about the price of your services.'*

In thinking about your career be very clear about what you will and will not do. About, in short, where you'd draw the line. About what you would not do however much they paid you.

Get yourself a mentor

This may sound a bit grand for some folk but I love this quote from Hellerman and Joli who worked for the Cambridge International Group. This first appeared on Fast Company (**www.fastcompany.com**).

> *Studies have repeatedly demonstrated that mentoring is the single most valuable ingredient in a successful career.*

And that's because having someone to confide in and talk to can remove a lot of stress from your life, allowing you to work things out. It can accelerate progress and stop you making esteem-blocking mistakes. Another brain and another conscience are useful things to have.

When it really comes to the crunch – if for instance you are going after a big promotion or salary increase, or if you are under threat in your job – good mentoring can make a big difference to whether you succeed or not.

good mentoring can make a big difference to whether you succeed or not

So how do you get a mentor? There are three ways.

1   Look under the various organisations you'll find under 'mentoring' on the Web. You'll get an idea of what's out there but it's a bit hit and miss, like looking under 'restaurants' for somewhere to eat. But it may improve your understanding of the topic.

2 Go through the Prince's Trust, Business Link or your local Chamber of Commerce to get a list of possible local mentors.

3 Best of all ask someone whom you rate, someone at work or in HR or Learning and Development, who'll point you in a useful direction. A personal recommendation is best. Not all mentors are the same – the really good ones are exceptional, the not so good are, well, not so good.

Most mentors will charge and how much depends on various factors. Mentors for CEOs come more expensive than for more junior executives. If your company is paying, the fee will be higher than if you are paying yourself. Ask your HR people for help – most have a budget for such things provided you are specific about the help you need.

Understanding what you 'believe' is most important to you

I got this from Lane 4, Adrian Moorhouse's business – that's the Adrian who won seven gold medals at swimming in the Olympics, European and Commonwealth Games – who believes (and I quote from the brochure):

> **with the right kind of support, people can achieve excellence in everything they do.**

I told you these motivators were upbeat people. Well, I was invited to a session run by Greg Searle – Olympic rowing gold medallist. (By now I was a getting a bit of an inferiority complex having merely played club cricket and mediocre golf – you must have had the wrong kind of support Richard, I consoled myself.) One of the exercises was a self-completion one called 'The Self-Belief Wall'.

Your Self-Belief Wall

In the top two layers of bricks put the achievements or assets you value most in your life. Include both personal and work ones – your choice. In the bottom two layers of bricks put the characteristics that you think are your greatest assets. Then I'll show you mine ...

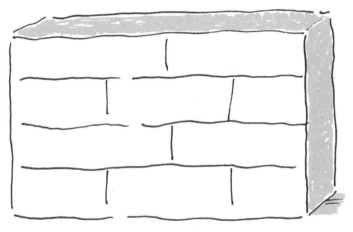

Your self-belief wall

Leading businesses	Inspiring teams	Having 2 great marriages	Writing six books
Captaining four cricket teams	Having fun		Making a difference
Enthusiasm	Energy	Reduced ego	Being a better listener
Not frightened of failure	Laughing a lot		Constantly discovering new things

My self-belief wall.

What was apparent in the group present that morning in the middle of a drizzly London was just how hard most people seem to find this exercise. Evidence, if nothing else, of how awkward many feel at lifting the curtain on their personality, their achievements and failures. Try it – together with the rest of the exercises – and you should by now be pretty tooled up in terms of self-awareness.

In memoriam

And now for something similar but perhaps less demanding. It's a good, if slightly morbid, dinner party game – writing your own obituary or, more simply, what you'd want carved on your headstone when you die.

◆ Spike Milligan, the writer and comedian, wanted 'I told
   you I was ill.'

◆ Tom Peters, the American management guru, wants 'He
   was a Player.'

◆ I thought 'He made others surprise themselves' wasn't
   bad. Nor was 'He made us all feel better about life.'

So you get the idea.

Focus on the one thing you want to reach for and express
it in simple powerful language (for example, 'She wanted to
astonish the world as a singer and a lover: she did both.')

Do you know yourself better now?

'M' is for miracle – the miracle of self-knowledge. Here's the
checklist to get you from 'don't really know myself' to 'know
myself like the back of my hand'.

◆ Mirrors – what do you look like?

◆ Maximum capability – what are you best at?

◆ Mentors – to bring out your best.

◆ Manage your ego – less 'me' more listening.

◆ Marshall your strengths, achievements and self-beliefs.

◆ Must not dos – eliminate the stuff that lets you down.

◆ Many points of view – see how others see you.

◆ Memorials – what you want them to say about you.

Things to think about

◆ *Really acute self-knowledge gives you an unfair advantage in life.*

◆ *But acute self-knowledge is unusual. Most of us regard our bodies, and the most amazing computers that exist, our brains, as things to be taken for granted.*

◆ *Imagine you were given a Lamborghini Mura and access to a hugely powerful computer.*

◆ *Now give yourself the curiosity to work out how to operate both and the ability to drive safely – and you are in a very powerful position.*

◆ *In your own way you are that car, you are that star computer. All you need now is to know it and go for it.*

◆ *Know yourself.*

◆ *Accentuate the positive you.*

◆ *Eliminate the negative you.*

◆ *Amaze yourself.*

2

To be told 'you really look as though you know where you are going' is high praise

Destinations are really important places. They are, after all, where you end up.

HAVING A REAL SENSE OF DIRECTION is very important. Too many people lose their way in their careers; no idea where they're going; no route map; no compass. No idea where where they want to go – stuff just happens to them. But if you do know where you're going, your chances of actually getting there are hugely enhanced. Although nothing in life is ever that certain.

A parable

You've set up your life plan and it's on course. You've been promoted to the local board. But at age 35 you divorce your wife, fall in love with a Chinese girl, learn Mandarin, start a PR company in China, which is a great success but you get shut down by the government and get dumped by the Chinese wife. Inconsolable you move to Bali, open a bar, laze around a lot, write a book, become an evangelical Christian, get spotted by a TV producer from the States as you mix cocktails singing hymns and get hired to host an American TV series called 'Drink to Jesus' that gets hot ratings. You discover you are a millionaire. You start an organic ice cream business called 'Nice-One' that you sell to Unilever for pots of money. You put everything into a dotcom business called lastsecond.com just because it takes your fancy. It goes bust. Very bust. You go back to Bali. Write another book. It becomes a bestseller and then is made into a smash hit film. You are asked to appear on Desert Island Discs. You become a society figure: rich and rather louche with long hair in a pony-tail. You are asked to appear in a porn film. You decline. You take up serious golf and win the English Amateur Open Golf Championship. You give up golf. You re-marry, to a gentle girl who is training to be a priest. You start up a new church. No-one comes. It goes bust. You are less rich than you were. You write another book. It bombs. You start an organic grocer's shop called Green, Greener, Greenest. It goes bust. You put the last of your money into a radio station called True. It plays music you like, truly like and it has a chat show that attacks people and institutions that it suspects are lying. It does brilliantly. You sell it and buy an old people's home in Bognor Regis and run it properly. You become chair of an NHS Trust and you start teaching Entrepreneurial Studies at Sussex University. You get the OBE and then you die of a sudden heart attack.

Your obituary reads:

Richard Naughton 1956–2009 Businessman, Writer, Public Servant and Playboy

Blimey – all that life in just a few dull words.

How to get to the top (or wherever you want to get to)

I was coaching an executive recently who, when asked what her skills were, said:

> **Seeing the bigger picture, seeing what needs to be done, creating a plan, delivering a result.**

I asked how she used these in shaping her own career. 'Whoa!' she said, 'that's quite different.'

Having a career strategy

One of the trickiest little words in business vocabulary is 'strategy'. It's tricky because so few people seem to know what it means. So let's keep it simple – it means a simple plan for success, it means defining where you want to get to and then providing a route map to show how you are going to get there.

So, destinations and strategy are what any successful careerist needs. You wouldn't do anything important at work without having a strategic plan now would you?

Everyone needs a career strategy – everyone. It doesn't mean to say it can't change, because people change, things happen, ambition is often shaped by circumstance and life is unpredictable. Think of Richard Naughton.

everyone needs a career strategy – everyone

Write your strategy now under these simple headings:

◆ What do I want to achieve?

- money

- security

- power

- status

◆ How may different jobs am I prepared to look at and in what sectors?

◆ What am I most interested in?

◆ What is the essential me and what I could be? } *Take your time over these two:*

◆ What are my strongest assets/talents? } *they are critical.*

◆ What are my weaknesses?

◆ How would I sell myself in brief (the key plus points)?

◆ What would my bosses, peers, subordinates say about me?

◆ How well have I done so far (three examples of achievement)?

◆ What is the likely route map for my career?

- number of moves

- special skills

- extra-mural learning/courses

- milestone moments (say four of these)

Well, if you have now been through the exercise you may have a better sense of where you want to go and what it will take to get there. We'd expect to go through this and more in writing the strategic plan for a brand of beer or canned peas, yet in writing one for a more vital and important brand

– ourselves – we get awkward, embarrassed and tongue-tied. Why? It really is daft, isn't it?

Well, that's the 'head' way of going about it. The cerebral, strategic approach to career development and to making it happen for you. It's your own secret marketing plan for success. But there's a parallel way you should try – using your gut and your heart.

Dreaming and feeling where you want to go

Be very passionate and very selfish for a moment. (A word on selfishness.) Earlier I spoke about egos and the need to repress self-glorification. I believe that's right but I also believe we have a mission in life.

There's an anonymous quote I really like which is:

> *Our talent is a gift to us. What we do with it is our gift back.*

So what is your gift and what are you going to do with it? And I want you to have a blank sheet of paper in front of you. This is about what *you yourself want, what you really, really want* – not what you could achieve.

> *I want you to dream about how great you could become*

Other factors may get involved as you think harder about it. There may for instance be family or geographical issues ('I'd love to work in the States but I have an ill mother-in-law and my wife needs to be near her', 'I want to work for a small charity but I've got used to a rather extravagant lifestyle with a passion for opera, Chelsea Football Club and antiquarian books') but, right now, focus on *what you want deep in your gut.*

Time to say, 'I'm an accountant but I've always wanted to be a vet' or 'I've been in corporate life forever and I want to start my own business' or 'I'm in teaching and I want to make money' – time to tell yourself the truth instead of hoping you'll chance upon the ideal career destination by luck.

Here's a list of statements that you must respond to – don't think too hard – this is 'intuition' not 'brain' time. The statements will indicate what you most want as a career destination – just put them in order:

◆ I want money – lots of it – as much as I can get.

◆ I want to do as little work as I can get away with.

◆ My leisure time is very important – I work to live.

◆ I want to be happy.

◆ I want to make others happy.

◆ I want to do a job I love that enriches my soul.

◆ I want challenges.

◆ I want to be famous.

◆ I only want enough money to get by.

◆ I want to travel a lot.

◆ I want to work with lovely people who share my values.

◆ I just want to get a job, any job.

Or maybe you have no idea what you want to do.

Many people don't even know what they want and that's a tragic situation. Most of us bottle it when it comes to our careers.

In truth in our career journey we don't usually get to somewhere even as adventurous as Calais. We arrive at Dover and then scuttle back home again.

Time to spread your wings – go on – in the confines of these exercises there are no risks. Just the possibility of discovering a potentially wonderful new direction in your life. All I can do is help you make it happen.

But one thing at a time.

You still have to pay the mortgage

I'm an idealist but bills need paying too, so in the short term whilst you work out what you really want and ought to be doing, you may just have to do more of the same.

If you've been paying attention you probably have a pretty good idea of where you want to get to next, all things being equal. All things (of course) are not equal.

all things (of course) are not equal

Those who tell you they know exactly what they want to be and do may be deluding themselves so let's slow down, think and explore various scenarios. For instance, let's assume that you've decided you want to work in marketing in a fast-moving consumer goods business:

◆ Why?

◆ Is it your best skill?

◆ Are you better than your peers? (You need to be!)

◆ Do you have the talent to be really remarkable at it?

You want to get on the board of this company by the time you are 40:

◆ Why?

◆ Do you have general management skills?

◆ How do you plan to get them?

◆ As director of what by the way?

◆ And what does being on the board really mean?

And before you are 50 you want to move on and become the CEO of a medium-sized business:

◆ Why? (Better be a good answer!)

◆ What sort of company?

◆ And what skills do you plan to have that it will need?

◆ Have you any idea what failure will do to you?

◆ And you realise, don't you that your chances of succeeding are slim?

But I'd also be planning the epitaph on your headstone if I were you (he said nastily). Milestones, headstones, whatever – I'm just warning you that the higher you go up the tree the more likely you are to be shot down.

It's smart to be nimble and open-minded

Because you are allowed to change your mind. And you are allowed to (indeed must) keep on discovering new talents in yourself. A route map is a guide not a contract that can't ever be varied.

One of my favourite children's books is Eric Linklater's *The Wind on the Moon*. In it a recalcitrant judge makes a wrong decision and won't change his mind. Everyone walks past his house holding their nose and saying, 'He hasn't changed his mind today – yet again.' The mind seen as underpants – I love it.

It was John Maynard Keynes who said cryptically:

When events change I change my mind – what do you do?

So what do you do? You do what JMK does and not that judge. Because a strategy is only as good as the context in which it was established.

The story is a simple one. Careers in the future will be diverse and interrupted. Events will change things in a radical way. I believe most of us will have five careers: we may have more. Be excited by this, not frightened. This possibility makes the messages in this book even more relevant.

I think we'll replace the word 'career' with something called – well try this:

P2P – Pathways to Prosperity.

For most, the idea of a constantly interrupted journey is uncomfortable; the concept of a pluralist career where you do many things is disturbing. Read about Charles Handy's Career Doughnut to understand this. In the middle is what you do to earn enough to support you for the rest of your life – how you earn your money. On the outside is what you give away for nothing, what you do for interest, the stuff you love doing and the time you need to spend with the people you love.

Here currently is mine.

Now do yours as it looks now.

My 'doughnut' showing an inner circle of sources of income and an outer circle of non-earning stuff that makes me human and gives me joy

Create a personal route map

This needs lots of milestones because who knows exactly what might happen next?

Write a story, the story of your life as you see it now. Then construct a vision of what might happen in the 30 or so years after starting work. Go back to the strategy – this is about defining the destination you want to reach.

Let's say your goal, your ultimate goal, is to become prime minister, or an animal feed salesman working near home in the country, or head of equities at Goldman Sachs, or partner at Clifford Chance, or group account director at WPP, or complaints manager at IKEA, or corporate affairs director at ASDA, or fundraiser at Barnado's, or an easy-going civil servant in the Home Office (does one exist?), or a teacher in a primary school, or to have a job in a big corporation climbing that slippery ladder, or creating a new organic farm, or being a full-time writer ………………........………..................................
(Fill in what *you* want – or what you think you want.)

Now create a 10-, 20-, 30-year journey with various milestones.

Fine, now insert the following six events – the jokers that happen in life – at random moments in the 'life-plan' you've created:

1   You've been made redundant in a surprise shake-up.

2   You have a new boss who hates you – she fires you – but then again, you have a big pay-off.

3   You are left a very large sum of money by an aunt in Australia.

4   Your company goes bust.

5   You fall deeply in love and your lover says, 'Why are you working in this place at all? This is nonsense. Leave it or I'll leave you.'

6   Your miracle product is deemed illegal.

The point I'm making? *When stuff happens, change course.* And because stuff happens, be flexible.

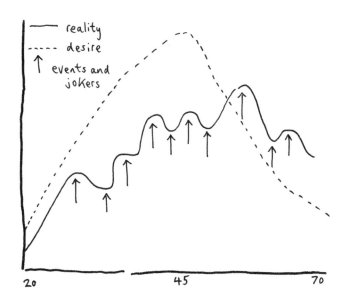

My journey through life punctuated by events and jokers (the desire was clearly to get rich by the late 40's and then retreat to the sun)

Hurray for pragmatism (which is just what you'll need). But an especially loud hurray if you've 'sort of' worked out where you're trying to go.

A career rambler is somehow so depressing. It's a wonderful vision isn't it? – rucksack on back, straw in mouth, crumpled map upside down, puzzled expression, greying sky, rain in the air and no idea at all of where he is, poor thing.

So here's your final action plan:

◆ Decide where you think and feel you eventually want to get to.

◆ Define the things that matter most to you.

◆ Set out all the things other than work that you want to do in your life and work out how to accommodate everything.

◆ Assuming you can't do what you most want, what would your plan B and plan C be?

◆ Have some fun – write a story of your life like Richard Naughton's (see the beginning of this chapter).

Things to think about

◆ *Working out where you want to get to isn't easy.*

◆ *But if you can manage it by thinking, by intuition, by passion and by debate then you'll be in great shape – and be very impressive.*

◆ *When they say, 'That young man/woman really knows where they are going', it is a huge compliment.*

◆ *Get them to say it about you.*

◆ *Have fun thinking about the options; life should be exciting and fun and your job, whatever else, is to extract the most fun from life.*

◆ *Socrates believed that our mission in life is to learn how to flourish.*

◆ *So how are you going to flourish, have fun, do well and be happy?*

3

Become a powerful learning machine

You need to keep on learning if you want to keep up in a global economy that's constantly changing and providing nasty shocks.

ANDREW MOSS, of Aviva, the insurer, said in an interview in the *Sunday Times* on 19 August 2007:

> *I have a high degree of curiosity. I love the fact that you can learn something new every day when you come into the office. That's what I enjoy as well as working with very good teams of people.*

Why you must be a learning machine

The idea of having to stay at school for the rest of your life, even of having to do lots of homework, may seem a bit disagreeable. But learning is just absolutely essential to getting on in life.

In our new knowledge economy it's obvious that we will all have to smarten up. If we aren't turbocharging our brains on a regular basis, we'll lose out to our global competitors who seem to find working very hard and improving their skills a lot less disagreeable than many of us seem to find it.

Whilst comparisons between work performance country by country used to be quite difficult, now we cross continents to find better value or better quality with ease.

let's start with getting our smarts even smarter

But being clever is not enough – it never was – it's all about your energy, stability and grace as well. But let's start with getting our smarts even smarter.

Why being a learning fanatic earns you more money

Employers pay for skills. MBAs earn more, graduates earn more, people who go on management courses earn more.

Whatever your job, be it marketing, HR, finance or whatever, ask yourself if you are up to speed with the latest developments or theories in the field. If you are, you'll enhance your employability.

Are you spending enough time listening to bright people who are expert in their subjects – at conferences, at lectures or in meetings? Are you reading the key magazines in your field and a variety of business books? Have you thought of getting new qualifications? An MBA may seem a daunting thought but consider it. If you can't do it any other way, do it through the Open University.

Fill your brain with new stuff on the key areas of concern that impact on any business.

Starting to think like a 'learner'

Here are a few examples of the things that influence and shape modern business lives. We all need to learn from them if we are to be perceived as good material by the puppet masters who promote people in companies or ensure they are spared in a round of redundancies.

The chances of improving our ability to contribute at our place of work grow the more we know. It's that simple.

- **The environment** – are the Greens right and what does this mean to our business? Are we seriously going to invest in bigger and better when the evidence says 'slow down' – what's your view and have you read the material that informs you? How should the debate where you work be shaping up?

- **Change management** – how do you make change happen? How do you reinvent businesses? Read Welch, Peters, Collins or Fast Company. Learn how to manage a change programme. Ask those who have managed one how they did it. Create a change debate in your workplace. What might change look like? Experience shows whilst things change faster, people change more slowly than you might expect.

- **Creativity** – are you creative? Have you been to a creativity workshop? Have you read *Brilliant Business Creativity* which I wrote to show how to make workshops work? Think about creativity – look at ads and at packaging design. Look at shop windows. When does creativity sing to you and make you feel dizzy? Creativity should be like a bolt of lightning when you make a magical and a previously unthought-of connection. You may not be able to learn how to be a great novelist but everyone can and must learn to sharpen their ability to see patterns and make connections. Just thinking and reading about creativity will give you a competitive edge. Incidentally, read (or rather browse) the best book ever written on design by Beryl McAlhone and David Stuart – *A Smile in the Mind*. What a great title.

◆ **Stakeholder management** – Everyone's talking about it, so be ahead of the curve and understand how to plot a map of networking opportunities. Learn how to create a stakeholder strategy by talking to an NGO or a good charity. Realise as you do this how many different people and groups you interact with in your business and how important it is to talk to all of them.

◆ **Strategy** – see the debate on 'strategy' in Chapter 2. If you aren't a student of strategy you'll miss out on being a high flyer in your organisation. Well, do you want to be a high flyer? Learn more about it by reading the Harvard Book on *Strategy* or look at Johnson and Scholes' *Exploring Corporate Strategy* on the Web. Strategists are often chess players. Do you play chess? If not you can still be strategically adept by working out what drives your business and makes it different.

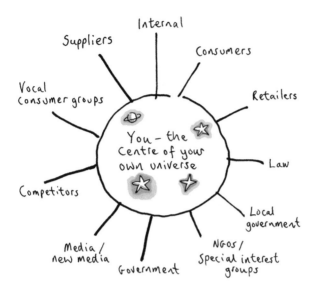

Internal

Suppliers

Consumers

Vocal
Consumer groups

Retailers

You – the
Centre of your
own universe

Law

Competitors

Local
government

Media /
new media

NGOs /
Special interest
groups

Government

Just a few of the stakeholders an average
Marketing executive might interact with
in an average day

◆ **Execution** – Harvard Business School has been the guru
of strategy for years. Now it's changed its tune and has
started to espouse excellence of execution as the real key
to business success. As the old jazz and then pop song
puts it, 'It ain't what you do it's the way that you do it –
that's what brings results.' Learn how to become an
excellent project manager and you'll always be fully
occupied. The world needs them. Learn the practice – on
the job – but also learn the theory. Read *Brilliant Project
Management* by Stephen Barker. Talk to project managers,
especially in big businesses like the NHS or major
building projects.

◆ **How to do what you do faster, better and cheaper** – this is really about engineering. Learn how to see your business as though it were an architectural structure with interdependent elements. Learn how the Chinese model (the 'do it faster, cheaper, better' way) could actually work for you. Learn how to re-engineer your business and, while you're at it, your life. Could you learn how to apply this to your day-to-day living?

◆ **Presentation skills** – I teach executives how to present the whole time and the more people do it the better they get. It's that simple. You can't learn to be good at anything until you try it, fail, try again, get a bit better, try again, have a catastrophe, try again, try again, be brilliant, try again, be really brilliant, try again, have a bit of a disaster (no-one should ever get too big for their boots). You *learn* to be a presenter; it is not a gift from God. And you're only as good as the last presentation you did. Read *Brilliant Presentation* for useful tips.

◆ **Talent development** – this is one of the big topics of conversation in many companies nowadays. When the flow of information is so fast and universal and the processes of engineering design so common and ubiquitous, being different is difficult. Yet it is by being different that companies stay ahead of their competitors. The key way of achieving such difference is through bringing on the talent in your company – by helping your best people learn how to be better. Learning how to make talent flourish may be the biggest skill in business today. This insight impacts on everyone. Since talent and the refinement and development of talent is seen as so vital, make sure you are in that talent pool. But remember it is more important to be smart and a team player than it is to be clever. EQ (emotional quotient) is more important than IQ (intelligence quotient).

◆ **Leadership** – everyone's talking about the value of great leadership whether it is in football, rugby, cricket, politics or business. Even if you plan to be a follower rather than a leader, or even a highly paid skiver, you need to learn what the key skills of leadership are seen to be. At the very least this means you can understand why your top managers behave as they do.

◆ **Communications** – used to be easy to understand – ITV, Radio Luxembourg, *Woman's Own*, *Punch*, a few papers and poster sites. Then along came 200 TV channels, the Web, advertising sites everywhere – even on animals (would you believe there was a guy in New York who stencilled a brand name on to pigeons' breasts?). We poor consumers all suffer from 'promotional overload'. So what's to learn? Well, if you are anywhere near a commercial operation you need to know how this new world of reaching consumers works. No longer is it good enough to talk about the media, when an angry blog or complaint on the Web can undo months of planned promotion by an advertiser. If you aren't attuned to the new media world you aren't alive to the opportunities and risks of today's world.

This list could go on and on. Even without having an MBA, having clear and strong views on the above will take you to new places in terms of promotion and you'll be identified as a coming talent in your organisation.

you'll be identified as a coming talent in your organisation

Seeming keen to get on by developing your brainpower is an attractive feature in any employee

A word constantly being used nowadays is 'sticky'. It means something or someone having the adhesive quality whereby they attract things to them. It used to be 'magnetic', now it's 'sticky' – same thing, just a more folksy feel.

Do you have that sense of curiosity whereby you build up a library of ideas, thoughts and images as you walk around during the day? Do you have a sticky mind? Are you an early adopter of new thoughts? Do you go to new shops and restaurants? Do you enjoy new things?

You'd better be sticky. In a world changing as fast as ours is, to be conservative and averse to change is foolish and will impede your career. You have to love change if you are to have any chance of getting on.

Write down the six most exciting new products you've used or come across in the past couple of years. From i-pad to Sheila's Wheels, the motor insurer for women, from My Hotel to the Pod in New York to Aerogel, otherwise known as 'Frozen Smoke' (it can withstand the direct blast of 1kg of dynamite, protect against the heat of a blowtorch to 1,300°C; it's used in tennis rackets to stiffen them; it acts as a sponge drawing out pollution from water and it's only marginally heavier than air) – each of these products are exciting or will change our social framework in their own way.

Learn something new or improve at doing something every month

There is a real effort of will required here. You have to manage your time to do it and actually want to do it.

Learn to negotiate – save money – earn brownie points

Negotiation is really hard for many – so go on a course. Learn how to do it. It's a really hard technique which like swimming (at least for many of us) no-one actually teaches us. You can just pick it up but you'll waste time and opportunities in the meantime. You need to get really good. Talk to a buyer from any retail group and ask them how they learned to negotiate and what they advise you to do.

It's learning the simple stuff that makes the real difference

The stuff where you score is in delivery, report writing, presentations or time management – simple stuff. If golf were the metaphor for work then improving your putting would be the place to start. Anyone who plays golf knows that if you were a better putter your handicap would improve dramatically yet the part of golf we all virtually ignore is the only part at which any six-year-old could be better than us – putting. So learn to focus on the things that really make a difference.

Learn how to say 'no'

We've all had that moment: 'I was thinking "no" but my mouth said "yes".' Learn how to say 'no' nicely. The hardest thing in the world for most people is to say 'no' or indeed to make any negative utterance. If you are to progress you'd better learn how to deliver the smiling, decisive 'no'.

Learn how to be an extractor of information

For instance by listening actively, an exercise you can do with a friend. Each of you speaks for three minutes on a subject that interests you and the respondent listens and tries to encourage the speaker through an effort of will, positive body language and enthusiasm to excel, to excite and to inspire. Learn how to be a massive information extractor.

Learn how to change gear and do stuff faster

You need to learn how to do what you do much faster. Because speed equals productivity equals cost saving. I know some really bright people who do great work but are a bit slower than their employers would like. One of them actually got fired for not handling enough calls an hour on a baby crisis line for an infant product company. She earned top marks for quality of response and poor marks for quantity. One idly wonders how she should have behaved?

> *Anguished Mum: 'My baby's not well ... he's screaming and he's being sick ...'*
> *Call Centre: 'Come on get to the point. Hurry up!'*
> *AM: 'He's turning blue.'*
> *CC: 'I'm sorry I must time you out ... thank you for calling us.' Ping!!*

Learn from those around you

We've already talked about the importance of having a good mentor so we're assuming you'll have got that sorted out but there are some other ways of learning powerful tricks too – from role models, from bosses, from peers.

Who are your role models in life and in business, and why? Try to find out more about them; read their biographies. And study the great successes in whatever field fascinates you – Warren Buffett on investing, Jack Welch on management, Dave Trott or Trevor Beattie on advertising, Jamie Oliver on self-publicity, Steven Spielberg on creativity, Steve Jobs on design. You choose – just find out what their magic trick is – and it's often quite prosaic. Sir John Hegarty, founder of advertising agency Bartle Bogle Hegarty said, 'You can't keep your eye off the shop for a minute.' He is very focused on detail but at the same time is intensely creative.

Work for an inspiring boss. I can't repeat that often or loudly enough. Find a boss you like and admire and whom you think has extraordi- *work for an* nary qualities. Study them, emulate them, *inspiring boss* learn from them.

Keep a record of what you learn

There's a wonderful product called Moleskine. It's the notebook designed 200 years ago and recently re-launched. It's been used by Van Gogh, Matisse, Hemingway and others, and now it's being used by me. There are various sizes but buy the one that fits in your pocket and in it record quotes, thoughts, observations, new products that you see – in fact anything you see, hear, read, taste or smell that you find interesting.

Over time you will build up a library of stuff only some of which will be useful, but that which *is* useful will be invaluable. Part of the reason for keeping these notes is to compensate for the fact that we get out of the habit of learning.

Your notebooks allow you to start learning to learn again.

And what if I simply focus on doing a great job?

That's never a bad thing to do. And no, I am not saying they'll fire you if you don't have a mass of extra-curricular homework every night. It's just this. In the world in which we work, the quality of our thinking and our creativity will mark us out for advancement. Our hunger for growing our minds and learning new skills indicates we are a modern person. In Richard Templar's *Rules of Work* when missing a promotion which he felt he deserved he was told he 'didn't walk like a manager'.

You don't just have to walk like a manager, you must also think like a manager if you want to get on – and not just think like one but also look as if you are thinking like one. And to do that you have to be constantly learning new stuff.

Things to think about

◆ *Encourage those around you to learn too. Make the idea of filling your brain with new things normal.*

◆ *Be full of curiosity. Ask questions. Read. Look. Wonder.*

◆ *Loving to learn can be a big asset in getting on – it makes you look and behave as though you are keen.*

◆ *It also makes you better company and it helps make your company better.*

4

Rediscover the lost art of listening

Become an avid listener. Listen more than you talk.

The noise that's made us lose it

It happened with the advent of auricular multi-tasking – what teenagers do with such aplomb. They look at the TV, they text, work on the Web, talk on the phone, listen to music and do their homework, all at the same time. They have a breadth of consciousness we can't match because their receptor is on search the whole time: a 'search' for something better or different. In today's world, be boring and people won't hear you.

The art of listening has been lost. The art of hearing subtleties in communication has gone forever. Ambiguity and irony are being destroyed. But the need to listen still exists in business and you'd better be aware of how important it is.

But first of all how does this work as a science as well as an art?

The science of listening – the art of understanding

The hierarchy of understanding goes as follows:

```
        ↓
    Looking     ⎤
        ↓       ⎬   EYES
    Focusing    ⎦
        ↓
    Listening   ⎤
        ↓       ⎬   EARS
    Hearing     ⎦
        ↓
    Connecting  ⎤
        ↓       ⎬   BRAIN
  Understanding ⎦
        ↓
```

The science of listening and comprehension

That's why the looking and focusing process is so important. And don't just anticipate what's going to be said. Let it come to you … hear what is being said.

Once years ago I, to my chagrin, was responsible for the following disgraceful exchange:

Him*: Will you let me have my say?*
Me*: Why bother? I know what you're going to say and I disagree with you.*

Nowadays I try to be more receptive and hear what people are saying and – just as importantly – deduce what they *mean* to say.

Why your ears are so important to your career

Career success is going to be about just two things – how good you are at what you do and how well you get on with people. To do either, but particularly the second, your skills as a listener are crucial.

For some people, when they are not in 'transmit' mode, they assume this must mean that they are in 'receive' mode. Not true – it's more likely that they're in 'not paying attention' mode.

it's more likely that they're in 'not paying attention' mode

But to be a good listener you have to try really hard. You have to try as hard as this:

I met a woman a few years back who'd been trained at Procter and Gamble, a company which always had a formidable reputation for its excellence of marketing practice. She did in-depth interviews with consumers and had been trained to do these without taking notes. Apparently these went much better and with far richer content with no tape recorder or notebook. She told me how she'd been taught to listen by looking at the interviewee and really concentrating, and then she'd remember what they'd said, fully and accurately, when afterwards she wrote it down.

Try it yourself. For about half an hour afterwards you'll have an extraordinary and excellent ability to recollect. You'll even recall body language and facial expressions.

Learning to listen, to hear what is being said, to understand what is being communicated (and then to remember all this) is key to making progress in your career.

Why?

Because if you listen, and through this remember, then you'll learn and quickly become more adept at what you do. Because people who listen are more popular and better company to be with. Because listeners are always smarter than talkers are. (People believe listeners are also deep thinkers.)

Doing business where it's noisy is bad for business

Trying to listen in a crowded, noisy restaurant is hopeless so the myth about lunch being a great medium in which to communicate should be blown out of the water now. Maybe it was once, but I suspect more sales opportunities have been lost than have been seized over the crash of cutlery.

And then there's the classic: 'I shouldn't really tell you this and I shall deny it if you breathe a word but you should know that ...' interrupted by 'Gentlemens, gentlemens are you ready to order? The specials today is for startings the lovely poached starlings ...'. That indiscretion that could have helped you so much will remain unsaid.

> *'Lunch,' as Michael Douglas so aptly said in the original film* Wall Street, *'is for wimps.'*

Look into their eyes because it makes you focus

If you look into the eyes of the person you are having a conversation with, you achieve two things:

1 You will command their attention and exert some control over the agenda.

2 You will listen to them properly and you'll hear what they say to you and remember it much more accurately.

If you are known as a good listener you are a winner

Earn a reputation for listening. I was told recently that someone was having problems with their boss – 'She's always on transmit.' People on 'receive' are better informed because they are more attuned to issues and challenges. They will also tend to do better because, quite simply, they are more responsive to what people (not least customers) want. And this is true as a perception ... good listeners are believed to be nicer and kinder people.

> *good listeners are believed to be nicer and kinder people*

Listeners hear what you say because they can prove it

There is nothing more flattering than to give people to whom you've been talking feedback on what they said to you. It says that you thought they were worth paying attention to and, better than that, you actually remembered what they said.

Power listening means turning up the 'receive' volume

If you can talk louder you could argue (and I am) that you can 'listen louder' too. I call this *active listening* and it requires hard work and concentration. If you go to the theatre and limply sit there in passive mode, letting the words just wash over you, then the chances are that you'll drift off to sleep. Active listening would call for an upright posture, a really attentive attitude and wanting to hear what's going on.

The enemy to listening is already in your head

In understanding the process of listening, Dr Bart Sayle, who taught what he called 'Breakthrough Thinking' to many major corporations in the 1990s claimed we had the equivalent of a little man inside our heads called 'You're Already Listening'. He was a stroppy little fellow saying, 'Yeah, yeah – we've heard all this before – let's move on – what shall I say next (and when is it going to be my turn anyway)? –

Gosh is he still rabbiting on?' You can improve what I've called *active listening* by turning off 'You're Already Listening'.

Click; silence; no nasty little man. Now you can actively focus and listen.

How to deal with non-listeners

Look at the way politicians, TV and radio journalists, and senior company spokespeople behave – they all transmit. Many of them don't listen; they have made up their minds about what they think before the interview and they make every question an angry reproach.

'Now are you really expecting people to believe – and we've heard this all before although one or two of your colleagues have been saying something different to you and I can see that's worrying you – that under this government and particularly in your department things have got better because the polls say the reverse and you yourself only last week got pretty near to apologising on this very programme …'

Well, just try and unravel that, delivered as it will have been at about 250 words a minute. It's a form of 'When did you stop beating your wife?' question although a brilliant riposte might be: 'Yes, they should, no you haven't, they haven't, they don't and I didn't.' At least this would prove *you'd* been listening.

You deal with non-listeners by being very polite and agreeing with them (in part). The words 'you are quite right about that BUT …' drives them mad and gives you control.

Most of all you gain control because you are perceived as a listener with a good balance.

Applying this is particularly important when you're at a meeting. Meetings are the place where all the rules of listening can, if you're not careful, fly out of the window.

Listening in a meeting is like juggling eels

Nowhere is listening more important than at a meeting. Nowhere is the sin of the mouth taking precedence over the ears more evident. Yet being seen to be good, helpful and responsive at meetings can be one of the biggest possible career boosters.

meetings are battlefields of egos and prejudice – and enormous fun

Watch for everything that goes on. Sometimes what isn't said is as important as what is. Watch body language. Arms crossed – hostile. Hair ruffled – confused. Covering the mouth – probably lying. And so on.

Meetings are battlefields of egos, self-interest and prejudice – and enormous fun.

The guide to proving you're a great listener at meetings

This matters because meetings are so important a part of life that behaviour at them is career-determining. This especially applies to the art of listening and the speed of comprehension.

Be prepared

Read the papers relating to the meeting beforehand. Be prepared. This means you don't play catch up during a meeting and can spend 100% of the time actively listening.

Simplifying the messages makes it easier to follow a meeting

Write yourself a page of main points from the papers so you can focus on the key issues and listen harder.

Be in a good mood because you'll listen better

Geniality can really help you pay attention, however serious the subject. Bad-tempered meetings seldom establish anything other than raising stress levels. And people don't hear each other half as well when under stress.

Avoid point scoring because you'll be thinking about what comes next

Do *not* be a smart arse. It's so easy to become one by irritatingly correcting the errors of others or by putting on a Pooterish voice and saying, 'On a point of order, chair.' Point scorers don't listen except for openings and errors. Point scorers make everyone else's hearing deteriorate.

Don't be rude because it distracts people

Do not whisper to your neighbour. It is bad manners, irritating and makes people listen to you and not what's really going on in the meeting.

Don't be a boffin because it confuses people

And when people are confused they start rifling through the filing cabinets in their brain for information and stop listening. Keep whatever you have to say very simple, jargon-free and to the point. Think of the listeners and don't show off.

Listen, watch and work out what is going on

Watch what is going on and try to understand the interplay between different people in the meeting. Meetings contain layers of political intrigue. Who distrusts whom? Who is trying to impress whom? Who is a conservative and who is a risk-taker? Who's at risk? Who's on the way up? What is being said? What isn't being said? What is actually meant?

Talking shops are listening shops too

a few are proud if they manage to survive a 50-meeting week

Meetings are very often the worst aspect of corporate or bureaucratic life. Many people believe they can survive by performing at them and some seem to believe meetings are the most important events in their working life. A few are proud if they manage to survive a 50-meeting week, leaving some meetings early so they can go on to others, using their Blackberry constantly (which is unforgivably rude) and spending a lot of time kowtowing to the chair and speaking in a low voice to their neighbours.

Or they are the best aspect of corporate life where views are exchanged and challenged, and fundamental differences are resolved. When meetings are regarded as places where you can listen to your colleagues and hear what they say they serve a vital purpose in remedying the lost art of listening and of allowing you to hear the alternative viewpoint.

And if you want to understand the process more clearly then try this:

Listening harder improves your memory

The better you are at listening the better your memory will be because you'll focus more actively on what's being said (remember that woman from Procter and Gamble). Making fewer notes and paying greater attention will also make you better company.

The more I see you ... the more I listen

The most important listening technique is to look intently at the person who's talking to you – most critically look at their eyes and into their eyes because it makes them feel good and it helps you not only focus on listening to them but also on hearing what they are saying.

I'm a radio – think 'transmit' and 'receive'

Think of yourself as being in 'receive' as opposed to 'transmit' mode – soak up what those around are feeding you. There's a glorious advertisement for Berlitz Language Laboratories in which a young German coastguard with little English is put on duty.

> *Soon afterwards a distressed English voice comes over the radio: 'Mayday, mayday ... we are sinking.'*
> *He struggles to reply: 'Ziz is the coastguard.'*
> *The voice gets more desperate: 'Mayday, we are sinking, we are sinking.'*

There's a brief puzzled reflection from the coastguard, who then asks: 'And vot are you sinking about?'

Listen definitely equals *receive*.

Listening makes you an advocate for others

By giving positive feedback about your conversations with others they know not only that you were there and that you remembered what they said to you, but they can also see how they have won you over. Listeners become the most powerful advocates because they 'get' the argument.

Asking good questions makes the listening easier

You need to prompt people you are talking to as well so you keep them on track and get the best out of them. This is 'constructive questioning' – the reverse of what you often hear from journalists on TV or radio.

Listening is a springboard to advancement

The real trick in advancing your career is to understand what is going on around you. Listening is the means by which you get the information. But the real trick is to decode it. 'Getting it' as opposed to hearing it takes you to the next level. Good listeners are never smart arses. The ghastly breed of 'point scorers' can never be any good at 'receiving' as they are always poised to make a clever quip and interject with their own, better point.

be a kind listener and thrive

The dominance of media and the possibility of being on it, for instance being interviewed or appearing on reality TV, has persuaded a generation of people that they must be transmitters. Go against the flow. Be a good natured listener and thrive.

Things to think about

◆ *We were given two ears and one mouth for a reason.*

◆ *Could it be that listening is actually rather important? It could.*

◆ *And 'active listening', whereby we actually hear what is being said and what is actually being meant by it, can transform your career.*

5

I love pineapples: the state of enthusiasm that beats the blues

If you hate your job, change it or change your attitude.

MARY D. FOLEY, AUTHOR OF *Bodacious Career: Outrageous Success for Working Women*, wrote in *VAR Business* in August 2006 that Gallup found 50% of working Americans were dissatisfied with their jobs. Sky News a year later reported 'Grumpy Workers Hate Their Jobs'. The research by insurer Unum showed declining job satisfaction in the UK. Many people seem to hate or are bored with their jobs, although for many it's a bonus having a job in tough economic times. Be one of the few really determined to enjoy work and you might get on faster and further than you'd thought.

So when you wake up next Monday say to yourself 'I'm going to have a great week' and then try to make it actually happen. And if you are going to succeed, it will start with your enthusiasm.

Get that bubbling well of 'feel-good' thinking

Someone was talking the other day with so much joy about life, that they began to get to me in the same way that someone scratching on glass gets to you and also, it would appear, to the person next to me who muttered sotto voce, 'And pineapples are just so lovely too.' Mindless enthusiasm and optimism is not one of the career tools I commend. Satirised to an extreme in the *Life of Brian*, 'always look on the bright side of life' blind happiness may not always be appropriate.

But enthusiasm has vanquished the cynic. The day of the negative pessimist is over. If you find either in your company avoid them or, if you can, fire them without pity. People who make you feel bad are people to be avoided.

people who make you feel bad are people to be avoided

So here's a real key to advancing your career and really making it as successful you deserve to make it: be positive but don't stop thinking.

Enthusiasm sells but 'intelligent enthusiasm' is a really compelling quality.

Think of the occasions in life when sheer *joie de vivre* lifts your spirits. Perhaps at Disneyland but especially New York, where energy and enthusiasm collide.

Get that American way of feeling terrific

As a city, New York has a boundless sense of confidence and is full of the feel-good factor. New York is the only city I've been to which never feels tired, which has a sense of irre-pressible vigour. 57th Street where the greatest brands in the world have the greatest showrooms. Grand Central Station – oh beam me down Scottie and let me smell that food. And Downtown, that Prada store. Excuse me luxury, eat your heart out. And Balthazar: 'Sorry, Glenn Close, did I just brush against you in this oh-so-crowded restaurant … I'm Hall, Richard Hall … and this is a terrific place isn't it?' New York rocks in a way that laid back, understated and ironic London never can.

Think about the good things in America – the ads, the confidence, their willingness to go for it and their sheer hunger for life. Be more like this yourself.

Enjoy our world as a big and beautiful place

When you think global (because we are all global and we are all beginning to feel it now) it's hard not to be inspired by the sheer electricity of life, its colour and its diversity. And when an economic blip happens in China, say, then an economic hurricane develops all over the world. There really is no hiding place any more. Not even the poor old Cayman Islands. Two-thirds of the world's population live in Asia and 'Chindia' – as the combined might of India and China is called by the *Economist* magazine – and it's making all the running amongst the growth economies.

'Why are you so interested in China and India?' I was asked recently. And I replied that what I was interested in, to the core of my very being, was that the greatest story ever was being acted out over there, the greatest in the history of all civilisation, and that it could turn out either way, in triumph or disaster – but wasn't it incredibly fascinating and exciting?

So to help you feed that well of enthusiasm, look east and wonder at the great goings on there, look west and wonder at the US of A, and look at yourself and reflect on how they all might help make you even more enthusiastic, regardless of the economy.

Half of you feel smug: why it really helps to be a woman

I can wax lyrical about this: about the increasing importance of women; about how they control purchasing and thus they control the economy; about how 50% of all business travel in the USA is done by women; about why half the people reading this book should be women (because they are ambitious to get on and really make it); about how they plan more prudently and are much more successful investors than men; about how they can multi-task. Summary? They are smarter. They are (by definition) intolerant of historic bad practices (the fault, mainly, of men). And, as I've said, they make most of the buying decisions.

Here's how enthusiastic Tom Peters gets about women in *Re-Imagine* (2003):

> *It is my fact-based conviction that women's increasing power – with their leadership skills and purchasing power – is the strongest and most dynamic force at work in the American Economy today ... this is even bigger than the internet!*

So there you have it. Have daughters. And one other thing – if you want to deny any possibility of your audience disagreeing with you, try starting a sentence with 'It is my fact-based conviction that ...'.

Are you keen on speed because everything is accelerating?

Speed is everything. Olympic athletes, for instance, run faster and faster. Have you ever heard of a sportsman or woman talking about consolidating their performance?

And the ability to go faster and achieve ambitions more rapidly makes you feel excited and enthusiastic. It fires your spirit.

Since the advent of the Web we live in an instantaneous world. Is it better than it was? You bet it is. Someone takes a picture of his girlfriend, sends it to a friend and in a few hours millions are seeing it. There are very few secrets left. We are speed junkies. We have speed dating, speed reading, speed interviewing, fast food and instant cures for ailments.

we are speed junkies

Strategically every business in the world is seeking ways of doing what they do faster. So join the 'get on with it' brigade or be left behind. People are built to enjoy speed. Fasten your seatbelt.

Be one of today's people and love nature

Not to think green is to be out of step. Because everyone, it seems, is thinking green, although if I hear another person saying 'global warming' in a knowing, tap-your-nose kind of way every time we have a light drizzle I might get irritable. From Al Gore to James Lovelock there is a huge weight of evidence that we all have to do whatever we can to help arrest the environment's deterioration. But as the severe winter of 2009 showed in restoring the polar ice-cap in the Arctic to 2002 levels, nature has a wonderful sense of 'give-and-take'.

Currently CEOs all over the world are being judged on their performance in building share price and their ability to find and grow talent and, critically, also on their responsiveness to green issues. Find me a 'let's put up more chimneys and to hell with the consequences' CEO and I'll show you one whose days in the comfy leather chair are numbered. The best advice is to mount a campaign to do better – which entails travelling less, using less paper, using more light when you need it and less when you don't. Being a thoughtful green is going to do no harm to the career prospects of anyone.

Being enthusiastic and optimistic as a campaigner for protecting the planet might even make you realise how wonderful it is and how unnecessary so much of the waste and pollution actually is. But do not be a woebegone green – they are the very worst of all.

Enthuse about all the talents around you

But first of all death to the hierarchy (it'll be a slow death because the ability of the old-fashioned hierarchy to survive is amazing). We used to live in a world of triangles. Where the guy at the apex was the boss and those of us along the base of the triangle simply did what we were told. It isn't like that any more.

Today we live in more disobedient times, which is a good thing for everyone except those who want to be old-fashioned bosses. We live in a world where asking everyone what they think produces surprisingly beneficial results. We all know, for instance, that Bob in purchasing is a potential Olympic marksman, that Mary in marketing is a brilliant soprano who sings for a major amateur choir and that Veronica is a special constable. We all know that what people do at work is the tip of a wonderfully talented iceberg.

It is our job today to bask in and enjoy the skills and enthusiasms of everyone around us. The real fulfilment in life is to get everyone to participate so these skills are evident rather than hidden, as they so often are.

Cheer up – lighten up

Light is important stuff and we misuse it. We work in dark and dingy offices generally in light about a third as bright as it is outside. We are crazy. We are also going to go blind if we carry on like this. Intriguingly, according to Leon Kreitzman, who is the co-author of *The Rhythms of Life*, a brilliant book about the science of time, if we lift the light levels to about 1000 lux, which is the same as TV studio lighting, as opposed to the normal 400 lux in offices (that's the same as we get at sunset on a clear day) then we operate much more efficiently and cheerfully.

work in much brighter light

So there you have it. One of the very best things you can do for your career is to work in much brighter light.

10 Lux = Candle at 0.5 m
80 Lux = Hallway/Toilet
400 Lux = Brightly lit office
1000 Lux = Typical TV studio
65000 Lux = Sunlight on an average
             day (range 32 km – 100 km)

Lux = derived unit based

on lumen which = a derived unit

based on candela (so there

you have it!)

Lux - relative brightness of
where and how we live

Think yourself into good humour

From the beginning of the day when you wake up, to the time you are about to go to sleep, try to think positively. A few years ago I had lunch with an incredibly bright and interesting PR person from New York, Marianna Field Hoppin, and, as the conversation developed, diverse and highly opinionated, I realised we were getting trapped into that negative syndrome where one keeps on saying 'and another thing' and disappears into a plughole of despondency. Gang culture, economic meltdown, Afghanistan, Sarah Palin, Goldman Sachs, Greece and so on. So we changed tack.

'What are the five best things in the world today?' I asked her. Our mood changed instantly, just like that, and we found the five best things relatively easy to come up with. Try this yourself. It works. Here were our five:

1   The brightest youth are brighter and more sophisticated than they've ever been.

2   The dispersal of money, apart from at the very top and at the very bottom, is more equitable than it's ever been.

3   Asia has found its feet, triumphantly making this global world a lot more rounded and the West look slow and lazy.

4   Success in conquering disease has never been so effective.

5   Capitalism, whilst not all good as we've recently experienced, is demonstrating the power and exhilaration of choice still.

Thinking about the best that could happen, rather than being like the lugubrious Scotsman Private Fraser in the classic TV series *Dad's Army* declaiming 'we are all doomed', may have a better effect on your life than almost anything else you can do.

Think upbeat to get on in life seems good advice because the opposite is certain to fail.

Think adventurously and transform your mood

It is essential to demonstrate a little more enterprise to break out of the boring box of normality. This is what really inspires you to be enthusiastic and more attuned to the opportunities rather than the problems of life.

You do it by activating your right brain. The best way I'm told is to get a sense of where the centre of yourself is located, probably just above your diaphragm. Then breathe deeply many times and focus on this upper diaphragm while looking ahead with 'soft eyes'– eyes that focus on nothing in particular.

You are now in the relaxed right brain state in which thinking happy enthusiastic thoughts comes easily. And it's cheaper and safer than drugs or alcohol.

You'll find laughter is really funny

Laugh loudly for about three minutes. Nothing much seems to matter after that and the sense of liberation is extraordinary. Yes, you really will love pineapples when you've done this. Once you've got into this habit you'll start looking for things that make you laugh.

Use your sense of curiosity to have some fun and awaken your brain. Most of the time when we are grumpy or fed up it's because our brain has gone to sleep and we aren't being attentive to the bizarre things going on around us. Be an inquisitive sponge, keep your radar tuned up and start chuckling. Ideas come from what you see and the connections you make.

be an inquisitive sponge

Things to do when you want to get your laughter muscles working include going shopping. Walk around a few shops to see what's new, what's fun, what's interesting – new foods – new appliances – new clothes – new anything. Or you could 'people-watch' – at a railway terminus, airport, central square, large department store, a bookshop or a bar. Or if you are a bit more adventurous you could fly somewhere – anywhere – and compare the experience of being here with being there. In Geneva recently I was giggling at the sheer abundance of watch ads including one that proudly proclaimed the maker was 'a master of ambiguity'. Hmm!!!

Intelligent enthusiasm is fed by a sense of curiosity and a sense of humour.

You'll find losing control is hilarious

Hearty laughter makes you feel younger. Watch a small child laugh with that uncontrollable joy rocking them to the core of their being; laugh and you'll feel the refreshment of youth. You'll feel those cobwebs of doubt blown away.

In my first book, *That Presentation Sensation*, which I co-authored with Martin Conradi, I included an interview I'd done with David Heslop who was at that time CEO of the MCL Group. The chapter was called 'The Naked Truth' and it was David's advice to would-be, nervous presenters that they should rehearse stark naked in front of a full length mirror. 'If you can present like that you can present anywhere and to anyone,' he counselled darkly.

Someone took his advice. He stood up to present feeling strangely confident. But as he started speaking he recalled the image of himself as a tubby man completely naked, rehearsing the night before. He got the giggles. So badly he had to stop his presentation. And then he felt it only fair to explain why he'd been laughing. By now the whole audience was in hysterics. When they'd all recovered he started again. It was a great presentation brilliantly received.

That's what laughter can do.

Don't take 'yes' for an answer

Enthusiasm is systemic not skin deep. It doesn't mean being casual or not asking hard questions. Interrogate with a ruthless determination to get to the bottom of things in the certain knowledge that first impressions count but are seldom entirely right. The more you quiz someone – and when you do it, do it nicely, this is not the Spanish Inquisition – the more likely you are to unearth hidden treasures of talent or potential.

Good news often lies underneath a bushel of denial.

Get on with people and show an enthusiast's skill

Start by smiling at people because enthusiasm is catching. Mostly they'll smile back. So everyone's a winner. I did this to someone on a train recently for whom before this I'd conceived an irrational dislike. They had a lovely smile. I felt a better person.

And work at making those around you feel good about themselves; show the power of positivism.

Recently I was working on a team-building project with a group who didn't seem particularly attuned to the task. I made each person in turn sit on a chair in front of the group. Each person had to listen for a few minutes to the group saying what each member most valued them for. The feel-good that flowed from that was extraordinary.

by looking at the sunshine the clouds disappear

Astonishingly just by looking at the sunshine the clouds disappear.

Suns and planets—
a warm relationship

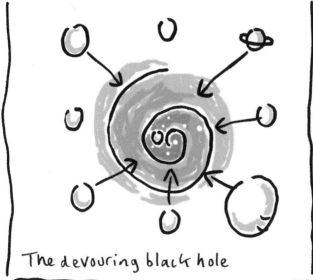

The devouring black hole

Are you a sun or a black hole?

But life is not all sunshine – unfortunately there's also something called 'a black hole'. The one warms and is life-enhancing, the other devours.

You will have black holes in your organisation. Avoid them. Keep them away from your talented people. Fire them.

Sadly the Black Hole Brigade often gets admired for its firmness of touch and ability to quell dissent. Members are in fact absorbers of talent and destroyers of potential. They may be good at creating tomorrow's headline, but are hopeless at five-year plans.

Use the language of positive thinking

The language we use will make a big difference to those around us and how they perceive us. Powerful can-do language is a big turn on. Withering, weak and sarcastic language makes everyone feel wretched.

Try and get into the habit of using positive non-blame attributing language.

NEGATIVE STUFF	POSITIVE STUFF
It isn't fair	Let's fix this
Isn't that just typical	Here's a real challenge
It'll never work	Let's see if it works
We've tried that before	Let's make it work now
What's the hidden agenda?	Let's go for it
Who thought that one up?	Is it your idea? It's great
It's not my job	Can I help?
They'll never agree	Let's try it out on them

Things to think about

◆ *Just by thinking positively you can change everything.*

◆ *Focus on things and people you like.*

◆ *Regard those implacable challenges as stuff to be good-naturedly overcome.*

◆ *Try having an amazing week of good news, positive thinking and geniality – and see how much better it makes you feel.*

◆ *You might even have a WOW moment.*

◆ *No. You will have a WOW moment.*

6

Help your boss and they will help you and your career

Give your boss the very best guidance, help and motivation and then see how much nicer your life becomes as a result.

Understand what your boss really wants and needs

If you really want your boss to do well and hope that they have a great career with frequent promotions and constant glory then you may be better disposed to help them. That's a good thing to do. So try to be a good-hearted supporter. The world of the kingmaker, the individual who is behind the achievements of a success story, is the world of a person who does more than can be reasonably expected and who spends their time doing two key things – being a support and an advocate of their boss.

Making your boss look good

This determines how valuable you are seen to be by your boss. Interestingly, if you get it right you may even end up getting their job ... if that's what you want.

Whether that happens or not, be sure of one thing: that you focus on the goal of being a great lighting man to their leading actor. Quite simply you are doing a really good job if you manage to make your boss look good.

Your boss has a referee's whistle

In fact let's not mince words here, for better or worse it's your bosses who will determine your career success. They are the referees in your football game of a career who can yellow card you, send you off and whose actions can determine or shorten your working life. In a nutshell, you are at their mercy.

insubordination plays badly in the corporate world

If you are one of those characters who always sat at the back of the class causing trouble, forget it as a tactic now that you have a proper job. Insubordination plays badly in the corporate world. But if you are like that and can't do anything about it – a rebel without a cause – well, James Dean, I have a message for you: get used to being a rebel without a job.

Your only answer is to become a self-employed entrepreneur with no-one to answer to. We'll come back to you later. Meanwhile go and stand in the corner whilst we deal with your more obedient peers.

Be actively helpful to your boss

You are there literally to serve your boss's needs and wants. This does not mean you should be obsequious but it does mean you need to be attentive and appear happy to do the boss's bidding. In the service economy world in which we live, this should not seem too onerous. Good employees and good bosses are equally hard to find. You'll enjoy being good, being needed and being helpful.

The people I prize most in my life and the employees I remember most fondly seemed keen on making my life less frenetic and took things off my hands that they probably did better than me anyway.

Be a pleasant, happy presence

Be the person whom everyone wants to travel with on the 'red eye'. Can you never be grumpy and short-tempered then? Yes, when you are boss and not before. It's sometimes very hard to do but take a very deep breath and say, every morning, 'I'm really looking forward to today and I'm going to calmly smile my way through it.' 'Calm' is such a good word. Be calm as long as you are energetic too. I had some-one who worked for me who was very calm. He was also very lazy and ineffective. At times calmness on it's own can get on your nerves – his got on mine.

Be nice to those who work with your boss

If your boss has a PA, make sure you treat them importantly. As long as you treat those around your boss with respect and good nature that will do fine. I have known people who, neglecting such support staff, found it to their disadvantage when life got sticky or a crisis occurred. People who know what's on the boss's mind are critical – forget whether they come below you in HR's grading system. In the end this is not just politic – it's good manners. And it can demonstrate that you are good with people – the number one, necessary skill.

Your boss is the best mentor you can find

Your best chance of learning is to regard your boss as your most useful teacher. They are likely to have a lot of experience and should be more than happy to share it. It's generally true that senior people enjoy being mentors and simply love having protégés – people in whom they can see themselves when they were younger. Ask them to teach you. Flatter them into giving you the most precious things that they have – their experience and what they've learned from it.

Follow your boss (especially if they are talented)

Good bosses are hard to find. Let's suppose you are working for such a gem. Try to follow them from job to job as they get promoted. Look at Steve Sharpe who has followed Stuart Rose from place to place but nowhere better than in his role as Marketing Director of M&S. Look at the relationship between Jeff Immelt and Jack Welch at General Electric.

Always treat your appraisals very seriously

It's easy enough to regard these examinations of talent and progress as being a bit of a charade. Nearly everyone at some time or another has privately wondered if the rating system isn't a poor copy of school reports. 'No detentions this term – well done.' Treat them seriously – try to get remarkable assessments. Remember these appraisals get locked in the HR vaults but they do get referred to. And if you do a 360 on your bosses remember they don't want to be pilloried. At such moments excessive candour will be unhelpful.

at such moments excessive candour may be unhelpful

Recognise what their weaknesses are

No-one is perfect and you will, if you are any sort of judge, be strongly aware of your boss's shortcomings. It's your job to do whatever you can to cover these up and make sure they aren't exposed to public gaze. One executive assistant I know actually locked his boss in the office to prevent him rushing upstairs to have a fight with his own boss. Another virtually did her boss's job – until she actually got promoted to do it for real. Life isn't always unfair.

Avoid bad bosses

If you actually dislike your boss then you are, if you are sensible, going to have to find another boss pretty quickly. I once had one who had many talents and was an adept operator in virtually every respect, except for one. He made me feel terrible and incapable of doing my job well. He didn't actually berate me, he just gave me this funny look as though I were a complete and utter idiot. The day he stopped being my boss was a day in my life as good as the Relief of Mafeking must have been. My self-confidence and self-esteem were restored and I blossomed.

Your job is to make your boss look good. Their job is to allow you to be as good as you can be.

Understand the rules of the jungle

The way corporate life works is completely baffling to many sane people. The one-time legendary Martin Lukes feature by Lucy Kellaway in the *Financial Times*, the TV series *The Office* or the Dilbert cartoons are eloquent satires on the bizarre activities of people at work. It is a world very often of posturing self-importance, full of jargon and stupidity. But like it or not there are rules in this jungle and the biggest rule is that the hierarchy works.

Your boss is your boss. They may be a friend as well but beware. Your boss determines your salary, your prospects for advancement and your happiness. Yes, bosses are that powerful. Don't labour under the illusion that they are reasonable human beings equal to you. They are not. They are your boss.

The trouble with friendship with your boss

I knew someone who ran his business like Nero. He was alternatively incredibly nasty and incredibly nice. He behaved absolutely randomly. Yesterday's hero was tomorrow's corpse. This was management by whim. It was disgusting but it did keep everyone on their toes. He got married (for the umpteenth time) and the wedding was on Christmas Eve. He made it very clear to everyone who worked for him and around him that they were (a) invited and (b) expected to attend. This created an exquisite conflict of interests with family, children and careers.

By all means be friendly with your boss but be circumspect. The rules of engagement are very clear; business is business.

Learning to lie for your boss

I spent a long time wondering if a book entitled *Lie and Cheat Your Way to the Top* mightn't be an assured huge success. This would, after all, be more in line with many people's experience than the alternative *Become a Winner by being Nice*.

But the biggest issue many perfectly lovely people have to face at work is when their boss asks them to lie on their behalf. The kinds of lie will vary in seriousness:

◆ He's not in the office right now.

◆ She's on her way to your place – amazed she hasn't arrived already.

◆ Yes he's reviewed that report of yours – he said it was terrific and he's going to come back to you – can you be patient?

◆ The month should come in on budget provided nothing unusual occurs – like (unspoken) sales trends continuing as they are currently.

◆ I can say this in a way that Peter would find hard to say, morale has never been better than it is right now.

◆ Carol is working so hard that she amazes me.

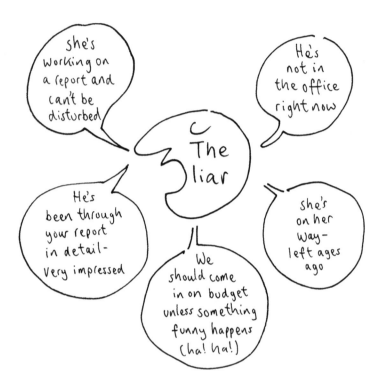

No-one should be expected to lie for someone else *but ...*
Occasionally, what the brilliant civil servant Sir Robert Armstrong described as being 'economical with the truth', in other words a fib or diversionary tactic, is allowed. He was quoting Edmund Burke in fact, who in 1796 wrote:

> *Falsehood and delusion are allowed in no case whatsoever: but as in the exercise of all virtues, there is an economy of truth.*

So the bottom line to all this is to avoid lying. If you have to say, 'He isn't here,' when he is, close your eyes and say, 'I can't see him anywhere.'

The magic chemistry of a great working relationship

When you have a great relationship with anyone, something productive happens. You feel as though what you are doing has a higher worth and that you are operating at a more effective and cutting-edge level.

What we are all looking for at work is that 'magic chemistry' and I'll talk more about that when I consider the essence of teamwork. But the boss–employee relationship is also really important. The thing about leadership is that it takes two to tango. The leader has to want to lead and know how to do it. The rest of us have to want to be led and be willing parties to the process. A great boss–employee relationship relies on this.

the thing about leadership is that it takes two to tango

It is, in other words, not just up to the poor old boss to be a good boss. It is up to us working for them to help them be good at their job.

How to say 'no' to stop it all going wrong

There are those moments in life where what is desperately needed is a messenger who brings the missive that says 'go back … what you are doing is going to cause you grief … retreat'. Well, we know what normally happens to messengers.

BANG! They get shot.

The trick is how to find the words and the tone of voice to bring bad (or less than wanted) news to your boss without them shooting you.

Here's how. Have a relationship based on trust, which you never abuse, so when you do blow the whistle they listen and realise that you are being helpful. Or tell them the problem 'offline' – over coffee out of the office.

Always give them a solution not a problem. Suggest how to get out of this particular problem or recommend the strategy of getting a bunch of people to 'brainstorm' a solution. And do not make the situation sound earth shattering. It won't be.

Your boss needs to be exceptional: if they aren't you won't be

There will be times when you work for perfectly nice people who aren't exceptional. But on balance if you really want to get on you will want to work for spectacular people who teach you lots and are inspirational.

Look for the first time ever on the barometer of inspiration – it's called the *inspirometer*. It provides the measure of how much inspiration flows from and is attracted to your boss.

In the end it's this ability to create an inspiring workplace that provides the magic chemistry I talked about earlier. Good bosses have this. If you find such a creature follow them, learn from them and help them.

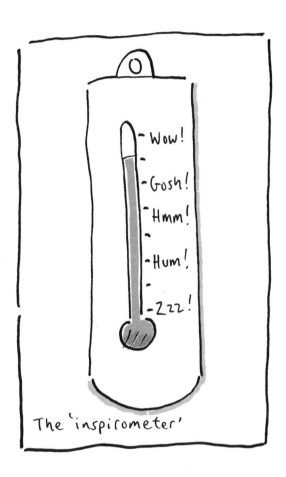

The 'inspirometer'

A parable

A sales rep, an administration clerk and their manager are walking to lunch in the staff dining room when they notice an old oil lamp on the ground. It's very dusty so the sales rep rubs it to see the lamp more clearly. Whhooff!!! A genie appears and addresses them. 'I shall give you three wishes. Just one wish each.'

'Me first!' shouts the admin clerk (first lively thing he'd done all year), 'I want to be in the Bahamas driving a speedboat with a beautiful girl.' Wwhhoofff!!! He's gone.

'Me next! Me next!' cries the sales rep, jumping up and down and looking as though she'd burst with excitement, 'I want to be in the Maldives with my young handsome masseur and a few of his friends, drinking pina colada and playing strip poker.' Wwhhoofff!!!! She's gone.

The genie stares gravely at the manager: 'Sir, it is your turn now.' 'OK,' the manager says, 'I want those two back in the office after lunch.'

Moral: always let your boss have the first say.

Things to think about

◆ *Boss management is one of the greatest skills there is.*

◆ *And it isn't that hard to learn if you are good at being one step ahead.*

◆ *Better still, from your viewpoint, most people are bad at managing their boss.*

◆ *They are unwilling and grumpy employees.*

◆ *So here's a real chance to stand out as a good employee.*

◆ *In fact, to become an indispensable employee.*

7

Individuals contribute, but it's teams that win

In the 21st century it's the best teams that win, not the most talented individuals.

Welcome to your new team

We've all been there, first day in a new job. You know, that moment of discomfort. You can feel them eyeing you as you walk in the room trying to look nonchalant. You have already in a flash made up your mind about a few of the people there. You don't like the one who sniffs all the time and Mr Egghead clearly doesn't like you and here comes Miss Bossy to make you feel at home.

Yet being part of a team is the reality of the modern workplace and being a successful part of it is vital to your career. Whilst a lot has been written about talent, rather less has been written on the creation of top teams. A lot of consultants have, for instance, focused on individual talent. But increasingly that magic cocktail of a great talented team is being seen as the key to corporate success.

If you can be a great team player and understand how to make teams outperform their potential you will be a winner and your career will flourish.

Team dynamics and team harmony – how you get them

Most of us would rather go out with some friends and have dinner than work as, let's say, a team member improving the 'Neighbourhood Watch' scheme or having an oversized meeting to discuss how to raise money for the church roof.

I'm not convinced most of us are pack animals. In our own minds we are still hunter-gatherers – wannabe Matt Damons, ready to take arms against a world of adversaries. But in a world that has become:

◆ increasingly full of risk

◆ increasingly female

we shall all have to put on a team uniform if we want to get on.

There is no choice.

Because this really is 'team time'

And the team dynamic, apart from calling for great powers of observation, is implicitly about singing in choral harmony. At this point you aspiring soloists (you are the bad guys) sit down and shut up, and the self-effacing choir, the *team* (you are the good guys) – the sort who 'want to teach the world to sing, in perfect harmony' – step forward.

So teams that work best recognise who does what and play to each person's strength. Teams are not just a mixture of individuals: teams are a cocktail of talent that blends together.

teams are a cocktail of talent that blends together

The top team – the theory

Patrick Lencioni in his book *The Five Dysfunctions of a Team* says in praise of the impact and importance of teamwork:

> *Not finance. Not strategy. Not technology. It is teamwork that remains the ultimate competitive advantage, both because it is so powerful and so rare.*

He's right. It is rare. He concludes that:

> *teamwork ultimately comes down to practising a small set of principles over a long period of time … teams succeed because they are exceedingly human. By acknowledging the imperfections of their humanity, members of functional teams overcome the natural tendencies that make trust, conflict, commitment, accountability and focus on results, so elusive.*

Is your team full of trust in each other, committed to a goal, performance-driven and do you all cut each other a bit of slack? Do you give and take like great teams should?

How being a good team player will advance your career

Given the power of the team to which Lencioni refers, every boss wants to have what they call a 'high-performing team'.

So if your boss thinks you can help make a team like this, they are going to be exceedingly pleased.

For a moment worry less about your own individual skill than about the skills you can help bring out in others.

The message is – know your role, know your place

And if you want to be a good team player help your boss build a good team. This will not be the most talented team of individuals. It will be a mix of types, but like the cast of the film *The Dirty Dozen* it will be the best you'll get, so get on with it and between you all make it the highest-performing team you can: the team that works best together with members who can relate to and read each other and understand what they will do next and when they need help; the team that makes the best of what it's got.

Can you read your colleagues? Can they read you? Do you feel you are meshing together or that they are holding you back? Is it enjoyable working together? Are you doing as well as you should be? Does everyone have the right role? Tough one – is anyone spoiling it now? Does it have a real identity? Is everybody up for making this team fun and self-fuelling?

We cannot all be superstars but we can all be good and, by working alongside others of similar quality who share our enthusiasm, we can combine to create something exceptional.

A really great team.

That, for example, is how a great orchestra works. They will all be better-than-competent musicians combining and enhancing to create a harmonious whole. I enjoyed the story about the London Symphony Orchestra which demonstrated how a team can perform. A fastidious and dull guest conductor so enraged the orchestra by his pedantry that they decided to teach him a lesson. They did this with a perfectly synchronised and unscheduled speed up in the middle of a Tchaikovsky Symphony leaving him confused, sweating, trailing and cowed in their wake, and of course the audience, not realising anything was amiss, thought it was marvellous.

That's a story of leadership usurped – proof that great teams can achieve miraculous synergy. And that great teams can drive themselves without having to be managed; that they can have a will and power of their own. When Arturo Toscanini died, his orchestra performed for a while conductorless in honour of him. The team is greater than the leader. Which given what follows may seem ironic …

the team is greater than the leader

You've been promoted – team leader we salute you

The stakes have been lifted. You're no longer team coach or cheerleader – it's now up to you to do three things:

1 Decide who's on your team.

2 Decide what you want your team to do.

3 And how you as leader will run it.

Choosing the right players for your team

Be a student of team dynamics regarding what works and what doesn't. Understand the differences in human temperament: those who work incredibly hard (burn-out material) and those who are very lazy (bore-out material). And then there are those who want to do it by themselves and hate being led by others (Lone Ranger material) and those who are naturally subservient (Tonto material).

Creating a great ball-passing, intellectually self-feeding team happens when you get the mix right. So be a team talent expert and recognise you will need to get your carrot and stick technique right. Not all people respond in the same way.

Rule one: diversity in your team will be the magic recipe

Diversity spawns creativity, nourishes the human spirit, spurs economic growth and empowers nations.

(G. Pascal Zachary, Wall Street Journal)

I love this remark. And I believe it's true.

Researchers once put a team of white, alpha male brains in one room – desperately clever men – to solve a series of problems. In another room a diverse and motley group were assembled, from professors to train drivers to checkout operatives, crossing race, age and gender groups. And – surprise, surprise – diversity won. Of course it did. Because it had more life and much more experience. *It had a mesh of knowledge not just a mass of knowledge.*

So in choosing your team bear this in mind. All men, all women, all young, all old, all white – any of these and you've got it wrong.

Rule two: why mercenaries usually make good team players

What? Surely this should read 'mercenaries make bad team players'? No, it's the whole concept of hiring the best available film crew and driving them to produce a great film. Everyone knows their part and is an expert. No-one has time to waste because time is money. You start at 5a.m. and you finish late. This is business, baby. So if you are involved in a shortish – a year or less – project do not be shy about hiring in freelance talent to help the team.

A film called *The Wild Geese*, released in 1979, featured the usual suspects – Richard Burton, Roger Moore, Richard Harris – and was about a mercenary army in Africa. The sort of film you want to watch on a plane, or when you're very tired, or when you're short of inspiration, again and again.

mercenaries get jobs done and then they move on

The message is the same. Professionals respect professionals and when they have a clear mission and the rate of pay has been agreed, they go and do it with somewhat more élan and purpose than a bunch of idealists trying to raise their spirits at a motivational skateboarding away day. Better still there's a start date and an end date. Mercenaries get jobs done and then they move on. Mercenaries know exactly what they have to do and what the rules are.

Watch your team at work

The dream team is in perfect alignment. But if they are normal human beings perfect alignment is a dream rather than a reality.

Allow for some individualism but aim for broad consensus.

Because when teams don't work it's usually because the members are out of line.

In the first diagram we see all the little energy and focus arrows that represent team members pointing more or less in the same direction. This is a team machine designed and tuned to move forward at a fair rate, pretty smoothly.

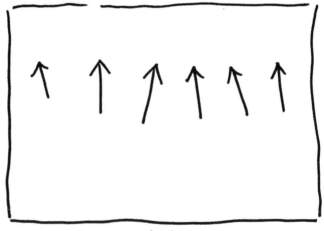

Alignment dreams

The second diagram demonstrates what happens all too often in teams. It looks like a nasty case of sabotage. Some are going one way and some are going another, all in conflict with each other. It's a perfect illustration of self-neutralisation.

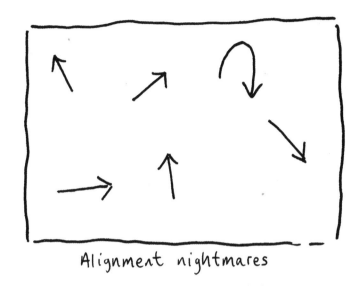

Alignment nightmares

More teams look like version two than version one in real life. But if you can get near to version one you have a high-performing team and that is precisely what you need.

Why is it that teams can sometimes be the force that brings out mean-spiritedness as well as encouraging great acts of nobility? Because, quite simply, many of the ambitious souls who work in the universe of corporate business can't bear letting those around them do well so they instinctively put the boot in and vandalise the team.

The important role of your team meetings

I've come across hardly anyone who doesn't decry the amount of time they spend in meetings. Meetings become synonymous with bureaucracy to many people. But that's unfair, because meetings can make people relate to each other.

Meetings make teams. Teams make meetings fun.

If you work properly together and you are leading the team well then you can create the magic of having team meetings to which everyone looks forward and contributes. When that happens you will also find that the output of the meetings dramatically improves.

Here's an idea of how your annual team meeting schedule might look.

Team meeting schedule

◆ **Annual planning sessions**
   (3 days off site)
◆ **Quarterly team meetings**
   ($1\frac{1}{2}$ days off site)
◆ **Weekly team meetings**
   ($1\frac{1}{2}$ hours on site)
◆ **Ad hoc topical team meetings**
   ($1\frac{1}{2}$ hours on site – whenever – say once a month)

OK, so that's going to work out at around 20 days a year when your team – mobiles off, Blackberries confiscated – are going to be there altogether, being an eyeball to eyeball team. Sounds frightening? Sounds to me like the only way to really make a team work.

Around 8% of the working year working together to work out how to hit your budget number and all the other stuff that comes into play at work, seems to me time pretty well spent.

Warning: there's no such thing as a virtual team

Teams thrive by the chemistry of interaction and I don't believe that one can achieve team dynamics by email or even on the phone alone. For teams to work they have to spend about 10% of their life closeted together and

teams thrive by the chemistry of interaction

probably at least a further 10% in informal sessions but with physical proximity.

Teams have to look into each others' eyes and understand each other. They have to trust each other, relax and laugh together.

To get on, be assiduous in keeping up with and being very visible to all the members in your team. Become that glue that makes the team adhere.

Fight budget cuts that prevent you meeting and working with your team members. Cutting out 'getting together' is like cutting out essential food when you're on a diet.

Think of your team as if it were a brand

People love being linked to and being part of a 'club'. Some of you are shaking your heads sceptically but think again …
They like being exclusive which, literally, means excluding others. They want to join gangs. They want to be in certain groups. What their peers think and what they say matters. Many teams respond to all the stuff that goes with creating a great and powerful action group.

Make a team video or DVD in which you make everyone look good and you capture the energy and character of your team. These things work. At FCO (and we were, after all, an advertising agency) we produced one so good that staff members used to watch it once a week (and sometimes more) and some said they'd cried (I personally doubt this). But it was wonderful I must admit. The point about these things is they get shown at home to family – parents, partners, spouses, children – and suddenly the value of your team of colleagues becomes clear and vital and a part of their lives too.

When you do this you make the team about more than doing a job, you create something with an identity. You begin to become a brand.

And then there's the rest. Get the team T-shirt created for the away day. Create a real sense of exclusivity. A group at the original Saatchi Agency did this by dressing up like the Blues Brothers, black suits, trilbies and dark glasses. My own group when I was working in advertising was loosely based on me being a John Thaw character and my team being the *Sweeney* (a TV programme about the Flying Squad with the immortal line 'you're nicked son'). Like Inspector Jack Regan, I kept a bottle of scotch in my desk drawer and swore a lot.

I must have been a ghastly role model … but it was fun.

Teams create their own language – choose yours

Clubs are exclusive which means to say they exclude outsiders. They do this in all sorts of ways, not least by the language they use. Have you ever noticed the language finance or HR people use?

I remember the first time I met some guys from McKinsey. I made a great discovery: *English is not their first language.* Jargon and hiding behind 'decks' of PowerPoint slides is. They are really impressive in their way. They teach you a few really useful tricks so if we are talking about creating *your* club then create a few shorthand exclusives of your own.

create a few shorthand exclusives of your own

> *Example*
>
> Call your agendas **menus**, call any how-to internal guide a **cookbook**, call any business plan or spreadsheet **the recipe**, call the debates on nice-to-dos rather than must-dos **stuff on the wine list** and so on – you get the idea. You could use Formula One or anything that helps you better define your own point of difference. And I quite like **kitchen fire** to describe a crisis.

You can learn more about your team members at play

Go and do sport together, do daft stuff like go-kart racing or orienteering or flying kites or hot air ballooning. In short, find out about each other when you are relaxed.

Regard the pub or the wine bar as an extension of the office. Use down-time as free creative time, as 'why not?' time. Relaxed time when the stuff that got vetoed or which seemed too difficult to consider doing in the sanitised air-conditioned office may spring into new life. Playing is something we all need to do more of if we want to be more effective team players.

You don't all have to be best friends but if you are smart you will recognise that people who get on together socially as well as at work will have a stronger loyalty to each other and work harder for each other.

Working for each other is what great teamwork is all about.

Teams need cheering up

Teams get jaded and wind down. Too many people at work indulge in something called 'binge-thinking' and get out of their brains on away-days and brainstorms and events like that. Too many people simply work too hard, to the detriment of all.

Your role as team leader is to ensure the team gets fed the right diet. Take the team somewhere new, for just two hours, to stare, to be aware and to get a buzz. I did this once to amazing effect by taking a team to the superfood store – a cathedral of fresh food – Whole Foods Market in Kensington. Some 80,000 square feet of delicious fresh, free range and organic food. It rebooted their brains. So get the team of which you are part to somewhere and something new. Energise people and amaze them.

The real and vibrant world out there is wonderfully exciting. Take them to the House of Commons, new Wembley Stadium, Canary Wharf, Stansted Airport, the new Bullring in Birmingham, the Royal Opera House, St Pancras – the best station in the world – and so on.

Your team needs goals; needs to measure how it's doing

Teams are not just clubs – they are organisations of people designed to achieve goals. So focus obsessively on achieving results. Be a leader who is always driving for more. My constant theme throughout this book is the rejection of mediocrity and not accepting second rate as being good enough.

How many goals should you set? At any one time more than five with maybe three sub-goals under each primary goal is too many.

Plus you need a team strategy and mission too. Something that the team members really identify with. As a rule I hate things like mission statements, which I regard as sanctimonious bullshit but in this situation you need one. Just make sure it's written in plain English and is very short.

Decide what you stand for. Are you change masters or process engineers? Are you creatives or cost-cutters? Decide and take a point of view. Decide on style as well as function – it matters.

decide on style as well as function

Team energy is your magic fuel

The trouble with many teams is they allow people to hide and cover up their lack of dynamism. They become 'people comfort zones' not 'performance palaces'. If you want to get on and have more fun then either try to work in one that is hungry to do good things (rather than simply exist in a gentle way) or better still become a leader of a dynamic action-team.

This should be the aim of every team leader – to lead a really good team. And apply the acid test about energy. If energy levels are low, levels of ambition are also going to be low.

The exciting thing about leading and being part of a high-performing team is that it gives you all the buzz of extreme sports. Being the leader of such a team pretty well guarantees you a fruitful and exciting life at work. It's a much better place to be than being a brilliant but eccentric loner.

> *Individuals win matches but teams and intelligence win leagues.*
>
> **Michael Jordan, genius basketball player.**

Things to think about

◆ *In the 21st century, teams are what you are up against, not individuals.*

◆ *Leaders are judged by their ability to help make teams deliver.*

◆ *High-performing teams are like brands – consistent, impressive and innovative.*

◆ *People want to be part of such teams.*

◆ *FACT: if you aren't a good team player you'll be history.*

◆ *FACT: the fastest way to make it in your career is to be a great team player.*

◆ *FACT: the way to stardom is to be the leader of a great team.*

8

'Are you being served?' Why responsiveness is so important

Responsiveness is the key to a successful and happy career. If there is one single piece of advice that should dominate your take-out from this book this is it.

JACKIE MOMS MABLEY, THE AMERICAN COMEDIENNE who died in 1975, said:

If you always do what you always did
You will always get what you always got.

She was a smart lady who apparently faced down the Ku Klux Klan on one occasion – so she was a brave lady too.

So, to be outstanding in this new world of service where the by-word is 'customer service' you have to be brilliant at being responsive. That means listening harder, working faster and doing what you say you'll do.

In the UK we are not yet good, let alone great, at service. Our current economy is being propped up by Continental

Europeans, many from eastern Europe, who don't stay long enough to embed the lessons of smiling and fast service into the indigenous population. But the lessons need to be learned by everyone and not just waiters and waitresses.

And this has never been more critical than it is now. If you aren't great at service, you'll be toast.

You will only win by being quicker on the uptake

When the customer says 'jump' then do it. The owner of Orvis, the fishing and now leisure outlet, distinguished himself by saying that the customer's right even when he's god-damned wrong. Orvis was right. To put the customer first – always – requires a mindset change. We are all in sales nowadays.

Why call centres offer so much hope to all of us

The hope lies in the fact that in the main they are so awful at response of any kind other than reading off a script.

being a great responder is actually pretty unusual

The competitive advantage in being great on the phone rather than just cheaper is enormous. Think of young mothers – remember that baby product company and the stopwatch approach they had; think of reaching old people; think of reaching any specific target group; think of a whole, new, friendly and interested way of responding to people.

If you can't sound interested in your customers why should they be interested in spending money with you?

We all have a big opportunity when the gap between doing it in an average way and doing it better is so huge. Being a great responder is actually pretty unusual.

Restaurants are the paradigm because they're so close to people

When service in a restaurant is brilliant the food almost takes second place, unless it's Andrew Fairlie at Gleneagles where both are peerless. Watch the best at work to see the responsiveness that marks out great service – places like The Ivy have great service. A waiter comes over and acknowledges you when you sit down, then shortly afterwards takes your order, writing it down as though it is a pleasure and with real interest, and the food arrives after 'a certain time' (that Irish expression which means probably about 12 minutes for the first course) that feels unhurried and just right. I read of one London restaurant where it took an hour for the first course to arrive. That is unresponsive to the point of lunacy (or, more precisely, it's commercial suicide).

Why we are so critical of bad service today

We live in a global economy where pretty well everyone has experienced service that is far friendlier, far more theatrical and far slicker than you get in Britain or France. The standards are going up, everywhere. The demands for customer responsiveness are growing. And you know something? That's our money they are taking – so too right that we are demanding.

Always remember who's paying you (the customer, your boss, your client) and respond accordingly.

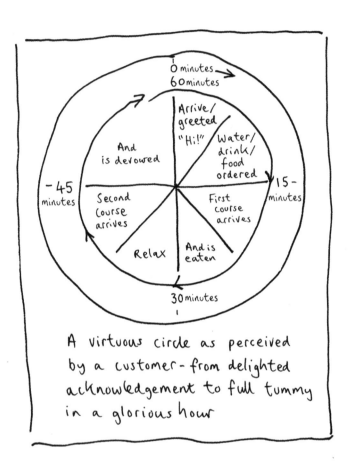

A virtuous circle as perceived
by a customer - from delighted
acknowledgement to full tummy
in a glorious hour

Commit and then keep your promises

Respond to your customers or to your bosses by telling them
what you can do for them and then slightly over-delivering.
Massively over-delivering would suggest you are not very
commercial. Most of life comprises of simple contracts
where delivery of exactly what is required is enough.
Nowhere was this better expressed than on Southern Rail

when a ticket inspector patiently explained the rules to an angry American woman travelling without a ticket. (Her point was 'I thought you were providing a service, yet all along all you want is to make money.') His explanation was very simple: 'You see Madam, you provide a ticket and we provide a train. That's how it works.' The rest of the passengers applauded.

Be on time – don't hope for the best

Being late is rude and looks sloppy. That's why some airlines make us so mad. Not only are they late they always seem to lie about how late. They seem to hope to sugar the pill by saying they'll be delayed by 25 minutes when you suspect they know it'll be a 45-minute delay.

Become an obsessive about being on time and about calling in even if you are going to be just five minutes late. Respond to circumstances by keeping others in the picture.

respond to circumstances by keeping others in the picture

Become a complaint extractor

Robert Heller claimed only about 10% of people bother to complain (although I suspect that figure has doubled in the last couple of years as we get more demanding because we get exposed to better service). Yet if you can get to a complainant and can actually solve their problem you may well turn a problem into a lifetime customer.

Respond to people at work as if they were customers. Ask them if what you are doing is good enough and how you can improve. Be on the front foot in soliciting what they think and what they need.

Care about what you do

I hate it when people 'busk' things because, whilst it may come off OK, it demonstrates a lack of caring about either the thing you are doing or the people you are doing it for. What you do matters. Your own treatment of it as something you yourself think is very important will communicate itself. Be keen not casual.

'I never have an email or voicemail that isn't dealt with'

Having a pile of unattended emails or voicemails looks sloppy and is a sign of terrible time management. It indicates a low level of responsiveness and suggests you are not very well mannered. Respond to the problem by setting aside an hour or so every few days and getting rid of the lot. Don't ever let the build up of stuff tyrannise you. If it does you will slip into denial and become a non-responder. You will be out even though the lights are on. The faster you respond the happier you'll be and the better you will be seen as doing your job.

Respond by ... slowing things down

Rushing around like a headless chicken has a kind of appeal to the speed junkies who sometimes pass for modern executives.

Try the reverse. Try to slow everything down. You'll find you listen better and that the person you are talking to will explain things better.

You are not in a drive-through restaurant. Try to create a more thoughtful and solicitous atmosphere. You'll become more considered and better in your responses to any given situation. And people will prefer you because you exude the most professional response elements of all – calmness and confidence. (As Lord Denning, one-time Master of the Rolls, put it: 'People pay us for our certainty not for our doubts.')

try to create a more thoughtful and solicitous atmosphere

Which would you prefer? The surgeon who rushes in shouting, 'I'm on a tight schedule, get him under so I can start cutting!', or the one who says, 'Good morning, how are you feeling? You know I was up early today listening to the dawn chorus: such a delight on a day like this ... it put me in such a wonderful mood. Now I'll be taking my time with you so don't worry.'

Good humour is the lubricant to great service

No-one wants to work with bad-tempered people. It's stressful and ill humour is catching. Try to be smiling, calm and good natured and everyone would rather work with you than your grumpy colleagues. Think of the people with whom you've worked with that you got the most from. Chances are they will have been the better-humoured ones.

Determine before you go to work every morning that you will be in a good mood. Your mantra should be: 'I will respond cheerfully to everything that happens today and with a positive desire to solve problems and accentuate opportunities.' A person who consistently responds like that has the equipment to get on in life.

No choice but to respond to change

The reason it's so important to respond to and embrace change is (rather like the air we breathe) we actually can't avoid it. It's also true that the very worst people to work with (apart from negative thinkers) are those who don't like or can't accommodate change. So become a dextrous champion of change and, more importantly, a responder to it and you'll do fine.

Jack Welch of GE said he thought modern business resembled a moving ball game. He then added that it was not so much a ball as a puck and the game was ice hockey: very few rules, very fast and very violent.

Being a survivor depends on how you've responded

With margins under continual pressure all companies need to reduce their cost base. And that usually means constantly getting rid of people – which means one day you too could be in the firing line. But so long as you are smart and cautious and responsive you may survive. Be seen as a bit sharper and quicker on the uptake and more responsive than your peers. Be the person they'd really rather not be without if possible.

So regard the pages here as a kind of body armour against a Black Monday.

Change and how to respond to it

Resistance to change is going to be a career killer. The world in which we live is full of demands for new business models and for workforces prepared to be completely adaptable. Your quality of responsiveness to what's happening out there will determine individual success or failure.

What we know is that the world will keep on changing and because of, particularly, the speed of communication the rate of change is going to accelerate. Do not let yourself appear 'irrelevant'. Even if you do not feel temperamentally happy with change try to be seen as a master or mistress of change and respond to it. In your appraisal you will be praised for your strategic dexterity and responsiveness if you project yourself as an apostle of change as opposed to an opponent of it.

Be the ultimate 'response-machine': be a juggler

If you want to impress then learn how to multi-task; learn how to juggle. Change masters have no problem doing this because they recognise that nothing goes smoothly the whole time: minds are changed; events happen that make good ideas suddenly become bad ideas; crises occur in China that make your best-laid plans redundant. To avoid this redundancy happening to you, you must have the dexterity to go, good naturedly, in a new direction.

Think the unthinkable: Destroyyourowncompany.com

This was Jack Welch's killer idea – responding to the changes in technology that threatened existing business models. When e-commerce seemed likely to usurp more conventional sales channels, he invited the guys in all his divisions to think through how their carefully built pile of bricks could be destroyed by a series of strategic clicks.

'you have to be paranoid to survive'

As a matter of principle, playing the 'how could they really get us?' game is smart. As the leader of Intel once said, to the displeasure of some who criticised his gloomy attitude, 'you have to be paranoid to survive'.

Ask more questions so you can respond better

Not like Jeremy Paxman ... or, then again, why not like him? Good, robust, challenging questions are the essence of healthy corporate life provided they don't descend into vitriol. Just don't take anything for granted and if anyone says 'we always do it like that' metaphorically put a paper bag over their head with 'you are history' written on it. 'Good, old-fashioned' is an oxymoron in the 21st century.

Improve your responsiveness – move on – move jobs

Every so often it's time to move jobs: because those lovely people you work with can't teach you enough any more or because you hate what you do or because you fear they are going to find you out or because it's time – you've been there too long and they treat you like the trainee (at least that's what they still think you are at the back of their minds) or because your sponsor, the boss that you really liked, has gone or because you fear the company is in decline and you'll decline with it.

It's best to move before they move you. Move because it makes you look like a winner. Always, always know the next move you'd want to make if you suddenly had to move.

Respond to the goals you've been set: then privately stretch them

Easy to achieve, well-within-the-comfort-zone targets are quite simply bad for you. Comfort zones are OK for cats but not for anyone who wants to get on. Setting goals is easy but achieving them is the trick and usually involves quite specific actions. Never have more than five objectives – three is better. (Set more and you'll only half do some of them.) Set yourself a stretch target and go for it. History suggests most people miss their stretch target but in so doing exceed their forecast target by several percentage points.

Avoid having a target (by which you'll be judged) that you and your team know is unattainable.

Respond to the chaotic world by getting in first

There was an old American TV police drama called *Hill Street Blues*, which at early morning roll call had the great line – how I wish I'd written this about our competitors:

Let's do it to them before they do it to us.

There's an old adage that says: 'If it ain't broke, break it.' I always thought this was daft until someone I knew had a blow-out on a motorway. He should have changed his tyres sooner. He should have done it to them before they did it to

*adopting the
'get-the-latest'
mindset*

him. We live in a disposable world. No-one expects their PC, their car or any household appliance to last a long time. In embracing change, it seems to me that adopting the 'get-the-latest' mindset is the one most likely to get you on in life.

Respond to change – read about it

If you aren't reading the seminal books of our time you should be. Try:

◆ Thomas Friedman's *The World is Flat*

◆ Malcolm Gladwell's *Blink; Tipping Point; Outliers; What the Dog Saw.*

◆ Ian Angell's *The New Barbarian Manifesto*

◆ Steven Levitt and Stephen Dubner's *Freakonomics*

◆ James Lovelock's *The Revenge of Gaia*

◆ P.J. O'Rourke's *The CEO of the Sofa*

◆ Richard Hall's *Brilliant Marketing* (self publicity is OK if what you are publicising is good stuff).

◆ Tom Peters's *Re-imagine!*

I guess that'll do for starters. Books like these really do change minds and make you think differently.

Respond to a changing world by going there

It is important to get around and see the way the world is changing. Here are just four examples of how the world has become a new place with new attitudes:

1   Go to Canary Wharf at 7p.m. on a Friday as the bars begin to fill and the whole place is throbbing with the sound of

money being made. It's the Mammon equivalent of St
Peter's in Rome, even now.

2   Go to Shenzhen just north of Hong Kong. It's described
as a Special Economic Zone. Fifteen years ago it was a
small fishing village. Today the working population is 17
million. It is rather bigger than New York with the fourth
biggest container port in China. In the centre where
Central Park should be is an amazing golf course. Just
outside the city is the biggest golf complex in the world
with 12 signature courses. Shenzhen tells you more
about Chinese growth than anything else can. Now a city
the size of New York is being built every year in China.

3   From the ridiculous to the sublime and nearer to home.
Go to any of the big cities in the north of England –
Manchester, Liverpool or Newcastle – to witness
extraordinary regeneration and the transformation of
the countryside. The north-eastern coastline used to be
coal black and charmless. It's now mile on mile of
deserted golden sand. From *Get Carter* to 'get that!' in
less than a generation.

4   Go to see one of the UK's biggest superstores – Tesco's at
over 125,000 square feet (at either Purley, Slough or
Pitsea). Is this the way forward or will we be looking at
lots of derelict stores like this in 20 years' time and reflect-
ing on the lunacy of town and country planning in the
20th century?

Change management figures large on the list of 'must be
able to dos' in any job nowadays. But even if it didn't I'd still

be advocating that you become a student of change because only by seeing how quickly things can alter will you be competent to read what is possible and what is likely.

The most exciting thing of all is that we now truly live in a global marketplace where what happens in Beijing today will affect Basingstoke tomorrow.

And you can't be any good at providing great service unless you realise anything could happen. A collapse in the global economy; the banning of air travel; a mystery global pandemic; the collapse of the biggest and best companies; the media exposure of role models. Anything can happen. But keep on providing great service and you'll survive.

Things to think about

◆ *Chances are you are a responsive person already.*

◆ *Why else would you buy a book like this?*

◆ *Spot changes going on around you.*

◆ *Be the most responsive person everyone wants on the team when a change programme is going to happen.*

◆ *Darwin praised adaptability. I am going to praise the ability to see the ball, decide what to do with it and then hit it further and better than anyone else.*

9

The power to attract

Law of the jungle, rule of life: look good and sound good.

WE NEED TO BE AS INTERESTING AND ATTRACTIVE as we can be to thrive and survive in today's corporate world.

It's a simple and brutal rule of life that attractive people will, on balance, do better than unattractive people. This is not to say I'm now going to propose you go on a course of botox or cosmetic surgery but I am going to invite you to undergo a self-assessment that is both radical and which is likely to prove lastingly beneficial.

Some will say 'no' to these questions: 'Is Barack Obama attractive? Is Gordon Ramsay attractive? Is Madonna attractive? Is Fiona Bruce attractive?' But look beyond the face alone. Look at the eyes, the self-belief, the inner conviction, the raw intelligence and their feel for people and the camera.

The magic chemistry

As we think about those people in our lives who have had that magic chemistry whereby we wanted to spend more time in their company, to bask in the warmth of their enthusiasm and to learn from them, we can recognise that they all had certain things in common. That they were enthusiasts with a great and a positive sense of humour; that they were amazingly energetic – a fizz of electricity surrounded them; that they related to everyone around them; that they lacked any sense of being excluders or failed to enjoy the company of what the post-war Labour Prime Minister Clem Attlee called 'the little man'; and that they were, to a person, great storytellers and great sales people.

Being attractive starts with your verve for life

Someone once said to me, 'Have you any idea just how tiring you can be – everything is so wonderful in your world?' Go and read the chapter on pineapples again and you'll see how positivism works. (Just don't overdo it, that's all.)

Look for the good in things around you rather than the problems. There are plenty of pessimists around who can tell you just how empty that glass is. Victor Meldrew, lugubrious star of the BBC TV sitcom *One Foot in the Grave* and his 'just typical' attitude to life was grumpy and a loser. We laughed at him not with him. Grumpy people are always losers, with Lord Alan Sugar a possible exception – although if he'd sold his

look for the good in things around you rather than the problems company for a lot more money ten years ago he'd be a lot more cheerful today.

Enthusiasm is attractive because it's a better state of mind in which to be than cynicism. It's a sunshine, growth and opportunity time when you meet an enthusiast. And almost everyone has the capacity to be upbeat. Find something you really enjoy and feel persistently good about – a piece of music, a painting, a book, a cocktail, a dish of food, a person – and use it (or them) as your 'mood adjustor'. Think about it (or them) and use it as the trigger to turn up your enthusiasm factor.

It's attractive to see someone fired up

It's not easy to be energetic when you're very tired. And that phrase 'I'm just so stressed and tired' is filling the airwaves at present with so many bright young people oppressed by their own work and lifestyles.

The expression 'if you want to get a job done ask a busy person' is undoubtedly true but it's also true that an energetic person's capacity for energy seems almost limitless. The truly amazing paragons of energy have marathon amounts of stamina or camel humps of energy which do not ever seem to run out.

I once wanted to run a coaching programme which went on for 24 hours, partly to see who could survive the longest and whether grumpiness or light-headedness won. Unsurprisingly I had no takers – but I got a huge amount of interest. I think in our 24-hour society, as author Leon Kreitzman describes it, the concept may have more traction today.

Build your energy by walking faster, setting yourself tough timelines in which to do things, breathing deeper, drinking plenty of water (dehydration is one of the greatest de-energisers) and by staying on the move even when you are in the office. The biggest single enemy of energy is the PC. People sit behind it and their shoulders slump. It's a great tool but no substitute for meeting, greeting, listening and talking.

Dynamos constantly recharge themselves. So be a dynamo.

Dynamos constantly recharge themselves. So be a dynamo.

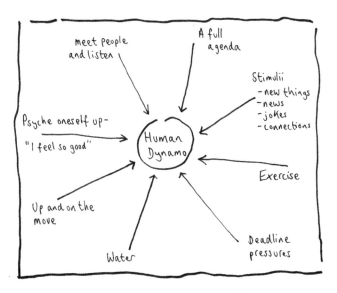

How to recharge the human
dynamo that is you

Be alive to what ordinary people want and say

The ability to relate to everyone around you is a rare and a valuable skill. It's what made Bill Clinton so potent a political force. What people who really relate to others have in common is a genuine liking of human beings and an ability to talk to them at their level but without ever being patronising.

How do you learn to be like this? By listening and by communicating the fact that you are interested in what others have to say (and do you know, when you behave like this, it's far more likely that they *will* be interesting?).

Most people are really smart despite the fact you may be prepared for them not to be. Some of us are marooned on an island of exclusion through our education, our perception of class or our status in an organisation. It's time to change that attitude if you want to be a people-person and get noticed as such.

So, get out there and start listening to what people are saying.

Being a great storyteller is attractive

And being a great storyteller is one of the things every great salesperson is. In Britain we are a little uncomfortable with selling – it seems so blatant and so, well, American (as if being American were so bad). In the USA, 9% of the working population – 15,000,000 – are in sales and $500 billion a year goes on sales salaries and collateral sales material and activity.

The Americans love selling. And you only have to read Tom Wolfe's *Bonfire of the Vanities, A Man in Full* and *I am*

Charlotte Simmons to see they are pretty good storytellers as well. Hollywood didn't get to rule the world of film by being a slouch at telling stories. Be embarrassed by neither activity. If you can sell, which is after all the single most important activity in any organisation, you are a huge benefit to your organisation. Salesmen who can sell well survive downturns.

In my book, *Brilliant Presentation* (www.pearson-books.com), I tried to help people become better, more accomplished presenters. *Selling is presenting with teeth.* Every presentation ends with a request or a demand for an order.

Storytelling requires the skill of being able to assemble information so it has drama, grabs people's attention and creates a surprise of some kind. The very best stories are nearly always written for children. Because the very best stories are told with unflickering simplicity and conviction. Because storytellers talking to children know their audience can always spot a phoney. Look at the extraordinary and beneficial impact J.K. Rowling and Philip Pullman have had on children's lives. J.K., inevitably being patronised by the world's critics – 'too populist and derivative my dear', is one of the greatest page-turning storytellers ever. She sits on the great storyteller podium with Enid Blyton, Agatha Christie and Roald Dahl.

More powerful language is attractive

We live in a world of sloppy language where we have stopped bothering to seek the clarity or the drama that engages those to whom we are talking. Our language now has interpolations such as 'kind of', 'like', 'whatever' and 'sort of...'; and – this one is catching – people don't 'say' they 'go'. I'm not just denigrating a generation of colourless talk but it certainly doesn't take us far beyond a small entourage of teenagers. Which is not that useful if we want to communicate to, persuade or even sell to a broad constituency.

we live in a world of sloppy language

How to be a much more appealing communicator

The advice here is designed to help you sharpen up your act, give your vocabulary the once-over and become an attractive talker rather than a mediocre one.

Less is more

Make every word count.

There are too many of them around right now.

Edit what you write.

Think in 'headlines'

Soundbites have a bad reputation.

Unfair.

Because they work.

Power comes from explosive, cryptic phrases.

So write short sentences

How short?

Like this.

Why?

Because they're easy to absorb.

And think in simple chunks of information

It sound simplistic but it works.

Always try to assemble your thoughts into three key points.

Try it.

What are the three key things you think about ... anything ... well, how about, say 'breakfast'?

Bacon.

And.

Eggs.

Social speak is not work speak

Listen to this: 'Like did you have a fab ...' 'Yes, er, we kind of took off and ...' 'Clubbed?' 'No chilled, you know.' It's full of body language, oblique and intimate 'we-both-know-each-other' language.

'Work speak' in contrast needs to be precise, needs to be

Focused.

Full of facts and figures.

A message that take you from A to B.

Something everyone understands.

Unpunctuated.

Avoid adjectives and adverbs; only use words that grab people's attention

They ban the word 'very' for journalists on *The Times*.

Leave most adjectives for poets and lovers.

Use power words.

Like: Crisis. Profit. Growth. Gain. Loss. Unique. Focus.
Team. Involve. Passion. Overturn. Attach. Defend.
Remove.

Adjectives? Hmm.

Negative. Positive. New. Powerful. Significant.
Transformational. Revised. Underlying.

These are allowed.

Because they are words that do things.

Words that evoke action.

Don't use jargon

We live in a world of jargon. Jargon excludes those not in the
know. Jargon also makes you lazy. And it irritates a lot of
people. Especially avoid acronyms. OK?

The drive towards simple, easy to understand English
will also improve your understanding of complex issues.
But try to understand the economic crisis by listening to
economists. Impossible. They are born to complicate things.

Me, I'm just off to the pub for a pint of Moral Hazard.

Use verbal signposts

If you are going to start a meeting, say so. 'Let's start.'

Politely stop meetings to give yourself and everyone else
a chance to sum up. 'Can we stop to check out where
we've got to so far please?'

Finish meetings. 'Let's stop now and summarise what
we've agreed and who is going to do what and by when.'

Communication starts with the eyes

Do you look down or away when you talk to people? Of course you look at them. (Just as you look at the road when you're driving.)

If you don't look at people you are talking to then you don't know what's going on, how they feel and whether you are reaching them.

And then communication moves down through the body

Your mouth – what comes out of it? How does it sound? Are you in control of the emotion you are generating?

Your ears – how many of us really listen? How many of us really hear what's going on? Use your ears to listen to *all* the signals your audience is giving you, not just the top-line signals.

Your face – what you look like (happy, cross, sad, excited).

Your body – what your posture says (calm, agitated, dynamic, poised).

Use all four if you want to maximise your impact.

Don't be a comedian

Unless you are one … and even then, don't be one. But do use humour to lighten the tone of what you are saying. It's been said that the great thing about someone who can be funny is you tend to concentrate on them in case they say something that might make you laugh.

Take your time and work in technicolour language

Advice from a sports coach (for golf, baseball or cricket). Do it like this:

Backswing: Slow. Slow. Slow.

Downswing: Quick. Quick. Quick.

In other words, don't rush the preamble.

Set up the argument.

Only start hammering when the nail's in the wood.

And don't be one-paced.

Not every sentence needs to comprise just one word.

Not every point needs to be shouted.

Listen to great preachers or speechmakers.

Soft *and* loud.

Slow *and* fast.

Cryptic *and* reflective.

They vary the pace and the tone.

All of them use 'splashes of colour' to reinforce and highlight what they say.

It's all to do with results not performance

Which is better?

'We played a blinder and lost 3–4' or

'We were awful but we won 1–0.'

This is all about winning and getting stuff done.

Because business is about action and success

In any meeting, in any communication try to 'move things on'.

What's the end game? What are you trying to achieve?

Always be the one who's saying: 'Sorry, can we get back to the key issue here.'

Be polite and encouraging

The two most powerful phrases in management are 'thank you' and 'well done'.

Never be rude.

Abrupt behaviour to some seems powerful.

It isn't. It's weakness.

It takes two to tango

Communication is two-way (or in a big meeting multifaceted).

Powerful communication is when you say 'A' and they respond 'B', and then you respond and so on.

Verbal tennis shows you are working well.

Power is in reaction.

And the attraction of reaction is it says human chemistry is working.

And finally

No-one ever performed powerfully without having a target to aim at or an audience to move. Powerful language helps define you as a 'do-it' person and 'do-it' people are attractive.

Why being good at thinking on your feet is such an asset

A similar presentation by two people of equal talent will often be very different in its impact and success, just as the same joke from different comedians will generate different amounts of laughter.

The key if you really want to be an attractive character is to stand out from the throng. And achieving this will often be the aspect of presenting on which we place too little emphasis – the impromptu performance and ability quite simply to think on your feet. Some of the most attractive personalities I've come across were simply magical at the five-minute casual chats.

simply get three points into your head and speak to them

These always seem tricky to pull off. But there's an easy way to pull them together at a moment's notice. It's called 'the rule of three'. Simply get three points into your head and speak to them.

1. Because
2. It
3. Is

Why the 'rule of three'?

Example

When I was asked to write this book a few things occurred to me:

1   **A wish**. I wish someone had written such a book when I was young. We were simply thrown in the deep end and commanded to swim. Quite a lot of us nearly drowned.

2   **If I'd only known**. If I'd known then what I know now I'd have spent a whole lot less time doing stuff I didn't enjoy or wasn't very good at. Like spreadsheets and numbers.

3   **So much fun**. Most of all, though, I wanted to write a book which was helpful to others, particularly in communicating just how much fun work can be.

It may sound extraordinary but this never lets you down – never. You just have to trust me and try it.

How you look and feel really matters

This is a totally pragmatic thing not a style or fashion thing. From now on in life always try to make the very best of what you've got including how you appear, how you feel about yourself and how you feel in yourself.

People will make instant snap decisions about how they feel about you, based on how you look. So there's a need to groom (that sounds horrible – it makes you sound like a gorilla), to dress and behave attractively, and to do yourself justice without being narcissistic.

do yourself justice without being narcissistic

Always look as good as you can and as good as you wished you felt without being too fussy. I pray for the day that men have the skill to look as good as the Italians who wear casual brilliantly. We, on the other hand, had a catastrophe called 'dress-down Friday' in many companies. Out came the baggy jeans, Caterpillar boots, Primark sweaters and Brut aftershave. I remember Fridays as being particularly horrible days.

Nearly everyone looks good in dark suits and white shirts. Cufflinks are very much in. Ties are increasingly old-fashioned. Hair should be worn 'under control' whether long or short. With spectacles – if you wear them – you need several pairs (for several moods and different occasions). And great brands work. Because they say to people that you care about quality.

Look after your clothes. Anything that's slightly past it or even approaching its sell by date needs to go to the charity shop.

Being a slob may work for Bob Geldof – well does it work for him? – but it doesn't work for many people.

Suddenly I feel chauvinistic – what about women? Friends say wear snappy, understated stuff that fits beautifully, in mostly sober colours. But it's up to you – you know best. Whatever else, spoil yourself and buy some great new clothes because you need to believe you are worth it.

If you are attractive to others you'll like yourself more

Go on a 're-launch' programme to get yourself in better shape, get a tan, tone up and dress a bit more interestingly – and see how much better you feel. And as part of this exercise throw or give away as much 'don't really need' clutter as you can – paper, old briefcases, clothes, ballpoints, books – absolutely anything that is bogging you down. Life without things you don't need is much more comfortable, fun and attractive.

The most beneficial effect of a re-launch is to make you reappraise your assets and your liabilities. It's literally time to have a therapeutic personal 'spring clean'.

How you look after yourself also makes a difference

I'm the last person to tell anyone to live a Spartan life. My favourite occupation is, after all, lunch in the sun. A perfect example of this would be in the Colombe d'Or in St Paul de Vence in the South of France, or in the gardens of the Cipriani in Venice, or lying beside the Loire eating cheese and ham and sipping Sancerre, or eating a wonderful roast lunch with noisy friends in Brighton, or eating Melton Mowbray pork pies smothered in Colman's English Mustard at Lords.

I can think of nothing better than eating a great meal in the summer with people I love, listening to them and laughing a lot. But the doctor in me says:

◆ Get to your 'right' weight. (Check on the Web what it should be and then see what seems to suit you – Digby Jones or Stuart Rose?)

◆ Drink plenty of water.

◆ Drink less alcohol.

◆ Do pilates.

◆ Walk a lot more.

◆ Work on your hair, eyes and teeth.

◆ A slight tan says you are relaxed but excess sun is no good.

One final word of advice – stress is not attractive at all. We love people who work hard but we don't want them to be white and shaking. And if that's how you feel, be like all the great stage actors who hide their appalling nerves on stage.

stress is not attractive at all

We are losing more days at work to stress than ever before – don't be a victim to it. It's only work: no-one's going to die (apart from you if you carry on like this).

This 'brand you'

Is it distasteful to consider yourself for a moment as a brand? Not if you understand what brands are and how they work. It can really help you, especially when it comes to the difficult issue of selling yourself.

◆ Brands come from somewhere specific and usually (thank you Mr Kellogg, thank you Mr Heinz) from authors who are very proud of them.

◆ Brands are consistent.

◆ Brands deliver what they say they'll deliver … always.

◆ Brands are worth paying a bit more for, not least because they have a reputation and because they deliver.

◆ Brands stand for something. Their designers had a vision in mind (think Anita Roddick).

◆ Brands have attitude. They can be uncompromising and take positions on issues. They speak in their own voice (think Nike).

◆ Brands are widely known.

◆ People talk about brands.

Be a brand. Think of yourself as a brand and see if this helps you focus on how to make yourself a more employable asset as you become a more attractive proposition. It certainly should.

Things to think about

◆ *Being attractive is vital if you want to get on.*

◆ *We live in a world of first impressions.*

◆ *So make sure your first impression is your best shot.*

◆ *Do a make-over; go shopping for clothes; get fit; lose weight (if you need to)*

◆ *Be positive.*

◆ *Be good fun to work with.*

◆ *This is the 'don't let yourself down' chapter in this book.*

10

Be a thinker and a doer and a magician

'In today's world we need impresarios and wizards.'
(John Sculley, ex Pepsi and Apple)

The needs of the new global economy

It's no longer enough to be only a thinker or a doer. You are required to be both. You are required to be a versatile master or mistress of every skill imaginable. Because this is Renaissance time in the workplace.

You are required to have brains, muscle, arms, legs, guts *and* intuition. As a senior executive said to me recently: 'Life in business is so tiring nowadays – I spend a lot of my time being a cross between a mechanic, a guru, a coach, a counsellor and what feels like a management athlete.'

So what does the average day in the life of an executive look like, not a CEO or some lofty being like that, but one of the throng of people like you on the upward ladder to success and extraordinary rewards? (By the way, I loved the account of 'a day in the life of Condoleezza Rice' who apparently got up at 4.30a.m. to work out. That's obsessive isn't it? Or is it becoming more normal? I certainly know more early-to-bed and very-early-risers than I used to know.)

The life of a modern executive

Everyone seems such a high achiever nowadays that it makes you feel slightly unwell. Imagine living with someone who says stuff like this in their mental diary:

03.30: Wake refreshed after two hours' sleep – create a PowerPoint presentation for tomorrow's meeting – phone my finance guy and am a bit vexed to hear he sounds below par and frankly sleepy – wimp! – I keep telling our people this is a 24/7 business. What's wrong with them? Do I have to do everything?

04.15: 30 minutes on the treadmill at 8km/hour reading the strategy papers and mail from yesterday as I do it. Fall and hit my head nastily when I try to read a complex spreadsheet as the treadmill programme suddenly takes me up a 1:5 incline. Think I'm OK – well OKish anyway – oops! I am suddenly sick. Must be that Italian from last night. Memo to self. Go on a fast.

05.15: William, my driver (a recent perk I've got), picks me up. As we speed into London I hit the phone. No-one answers. What on earth is going on? I text everyone and wait for responses. I read all the papers. I re-do the budget just for fun. I think we can save another $2 million just in headcount alone. I'm feeling a little bit woozy. Get a grip.

07.00: Arrive in the office for my team meeting. Where is everyone? Two members arrive 15 minutes late but look fed up and are distinctly frosty. I try to cheer them up but my head is now hurting quite badly so I close the meeting with the rousing words from Hill Street Blues *'Let's do it to them before they do it to us.' They look bemused especially as their other colleagues are now arriving to be turned away and are looking puzzled. I hear one say, 'He called this for 7.30 not 7.00 and he's now advocating pre-emptive retaliation as far as I can get it – "let's shag them first"… has he gone mad? And what's that gash on the side of his head?'*

08.00: I'm about to go into a strategy meeting which I fixed yesterday when my PA comes in and screams at me that I've double booked as there's a meeting on packaging that's been in my diary for months and we have people that have come across from Greece especially. She bursts into tears and says, 'I resign.' What's wrong with everyone today? Decide to run both meetings concurrently by spending half an hour in each consecutively.

11.00: Meetings end. Seem to have got through it all right but the guys from Greece insist I've agreed to let them change the packaging and the branding to Dionysus. Must ask what that means. Sounds safe enough and unlikely to breach our corporate ethics policy. Georgio keeps saying, 'What a great viral we can do – it'll be notorious' – their English is still a bit odd in Greece. 'Be famous Georgio, just be famous and keep it clean,' I say and rush to make the next meeting. My head really hurts now.

12.00: Whooaahh!! I am seeing double. A mild moment of panic passes when I suddenly realise that I can now speed-read two documents side by side. This is absolutely brilliant. It'll save so much time.

12.30: Our marketing team meeting. It's going a bit slowly so I decide to remind everyone we can really go that extra mile. I really inspire them … their mouths are open in admiration. My eyes mist with tears as I think how great the team spirit in this place really is …

13.30: Rush to the gym for a quick run – I must keep fit, I must keep fit – 'mens sana in corpore sano' – I eat a sandwich as I run – I've revved the running machine up to 10km/hour. A piece of cucumber falls out of my sandwich and I slip on it and bang my head again – suddenly I lose colour vision and everything goes black and white … Not my day. I brush away the help from concerned fellow athletes. I'm OK. I really am. I just have to get a grip. I've got four more meetings back to back this afternoon …

What a nightmare. And yet beneath this farce lies a horrible near-truth. There are some people out there working absurd hours; they're putting themselves under massive stress and causing absolute chaos for all around them. Too many people in work are having their lives ruined by manic obsessives. This particular joker makes Martin Lukes or Ricky Gervais look normal. One rather presumes (one actually hopes) he dies and his dying words are 'get a grip'.

Do not be like this. It isn't necessary or helpful nor will it do you or anyone else any good.

The modern world is full of fear and insanity created by stress. I knew a senior executive who started shaking when his boss called from the USA. Another who became almost incontinent whenever her German boss phoned. 'Bathroom,' she'd shriek, running off down the corridor as her PA said, 'It's Otto on the line; he wants to talk to you.'

So it's time to change the way you think. Change your priorities. Stop believing a cross between brinkmanship and speed-reading is the way to the top. In fact it's the way to an early grave and to widespread unpopularity.

so it's time to change the way you think

Have some fun

It's time to get human again. Remember humanity? Remember fun? Here's an advertisement for 'fun':

If you have a job at which you are good and which you enjoy, working with colleagues most of whom you like and respect, then you are lucky but you are probably doing more good to your company than if you are a workaholic.

Working in the modern world, finding new and interesting ways of doing things. Avoiding ruts and being smilingly open minded … maybe you'll do something really innovative … maybe you'll make a real difference.

Here's another advertisement for fun (less sure about this one):

Dominic Rushe, a journalist with The Sunday Times, *tells us fun is rife in a firm called Appriver in Gulf Breeze, Florida. They have created a cuddly toy 'attack monkey' who playfully 'kills' people at work and this goes on film onto their intranet. They apparently find this very amusing. His latest victim was the CEO who was filmed having a mock heart attack when he was presented with, and then read, the monkey's salary requirements. (Yes, you could see that might be droll.)*

Behind the mission to have more fun is a company called FunCilitators. They've discovered this gap in the market for 'fun at work' and, well, fun is really serious commercially. They've helped people like Anheuser Busch, IBM, Marriott, and the American Armed Forces 'lighten up' (oh please, the Armed Forces?).

The theory is this, says Gail Hahn, CEO of FunCilitators:

People need to have fun at work and they are finally getting it ... baby boomers are workaholics. Their attitude is they are lucky to get a pay cheque. Generation X have seen their parents work themselves stiff and still get downsized. They have been latch-key kids who have watched the sacrifices their parents made and they are not about to make the same ones. For them a life–work balance is hugely important.

From Gail Hahn's book *52 Ways to Have Fun at Work* here are the top four:

1   Create a surprise celebration and choose a Monday to do it.

2   Practise Fun Shui. Make your office multicoloured.

3   *Don't wait until deadbeats leave to say goodbye to them.* [Yes, I really agree with this one – deadbeats and Black Holes.]

4   Fill your day with 'energy inserts' – toys and playful items.

I really agree with play and what Faith Popcorn, the US culture guru, called 'down-ageing' but I suddenly feel rather old, stiff-collared and grumpy. 'Fun Shui' seems a bit too LA and flippant for my taste; or do they have a point? Maybe. Maybe not.

I'm not alone, thank goodness. One American consultant, Laura Ricci, confessed that all this blatant fun might have its downside:

I've been to twenty company picnics and haven't enjoyed one. They are an opportunity for career suicide.

This may – belatedly – be the best advice of all in this book. Avoid office events like office parties, which could be 'career suicide'.

Learn something new

Get out of your potential rut. Don't care what it is. It could be something that excites you: dinosaurs, roses, newts (good enough for the ex-Mayor of London), anything that grabs your imagination. Learning is energy-giving. It makes you an enthusiast. And it gives you a leg up. I heard of someone who learned a little Russian for fun and when a project came up in Russia their tender went to the front of the queue although the limit of their fluency was probably only as good as 'This charming city of Moscow inspires my brain with excitement. Thank you.'

Push yourself a bit more than usual

I met someone recently who'd set himself a golf handicap reduction target, which to his mortification he just missed – but what an improvement in one year. Do something that puts you under pressure outside work. Like how to become a world expert on something, on anything. By the way, world expert is an abused term – so use your nous and you'll find it surprisingly easier than you thought. Try being world expert on the street where you live just to see what I mean. Wikipedia has made being a world expert a rather crowded profession.

Become an obsessive 'asker'

Don't be shy and retiring; don't put up with stuff. Smile and ask 'Why' until you get an answer that makes sense to you. Start raising your own expectations regarding those around you. So many of us take things for granted. Start asking about stuff. Ask people in shops about products. If you aren't sure, ask. Become insistent on knowing what's going on. Asking how things work makes you a thinker and not a take-it-at-face-value accepter of things.

start asking about stuff

Start being ever so slightly difficult and use a vocabulary that begins to drive up standards:

◆ I don't want to be difficult but …

◆ This is disappointing.

◆ I know you can do so much better than this.

◆ How can I help you because you must be even less happy with this than I am?

◆ I know it's difficult but I know you can solve it.

Wander sometimes – straight lines are so predictable

And predictability is something we see little of in the world today. It's the detours in life that are often the most productive in terms of releasing new stimulation and ideas. Allow yourself the time and the licence to explore as opposed to always rushing to your destination. At 3M they encourage their people to spend 15% of their time exploring new and different things. Inventions come from connecting disparate things. Innovation comes from seeing opportunities out of the corner of your eye. I believe some of my best work is done when I'm dozing off — when ideas are 'stewing' in my brain.

Discovery needs celebration. Celebration creates new discoveries. When you discover something new or have an amazing insight, celebrate. Those 'eureka' moments are enormous fun and very exciting. Did you know that wasps love juniper? Did you know dark chocolate in small quantities helps makes a rich, dark gravy? That Kazakhstan is bigger than western Europe? That the Irish have found gold and platinum off Belfast? I didn't until a few days ago. But by using your ears and eyes you'll find life is a series of discovery moments.

Time to browse. Time to think. Time to open your eyes.

Visit places and open your eyes wide

We all seem too busy to do this ... to visit amazing churches, art galleries, cities, festivals, food fairs, supermarkets, new shops or

go and see things and refresh your mind

even the mind-blowing Borough Market or refurbished Ash-molean Museum in Oxford. Go and see things and refresh your mind.

Sit down and write the ten places in the world you'd like to see; repeat for the USA; repeat for Europe; repeat for Asia, repeat for the UK.

Read voraciously

The Times – James Harding and Anatole Kaletsky – they ring bells. Lucy Kellaway in the *FT* – she's a genius. Fast Company. Tom Peters. Patrick Lencioni. Check my own website (**www.richardhall.biz**) for links to the best on offer online right now. And dip into as many management books as you can stomach. You get some great material to use at work, great quotes and funny stories, but every so often something more important – a genuine and helpful insight that resonates with you.

Be alone, really alone occasionally and 'think'

Not for long and not as a persistent habit but try to learn how to think alone. Silently stare at the ceiling and think. Sir Isaac Newton apparently could sit and think in a 'blue sky' way for a month at a time. We live in a world of distractions. Learn to stop, focus and apply your mind to a problem. Slow down. Let new thoughts come to you. And eat an apple as you're doing it. The association may help you concentrate.

Carry your notebook everywhere

As you know, I use Moleskines because I like the feel of them. Nice paper. Useful sizes to fit in your pocket. Ernest Hemingway and Bruce Chatwin used them to make notes. What's good enough for them is good enough for us. Just doodling can unlock your brain.

I also like the idea of staring at a white page, which may be better than a ceiling. It's a great way, too, of doing those things you've been avoiding – that speech, that presentation, that proposition you have to write. I think Moleskine and its right-brain, creative users have usurped Filofax, which is a left-brain product.

Stare at that white sheet of paper and be inspired.

Life is a constant Q&A session

My wife is increasingly a bit startled to discover how often a drink in a wine bar becomes an interrogation from me. Not because I'm being nasty but because she's coming out with gems, things I hadn't thought about, things that make me think of other things. Your partner or your best friend can feed you great amounts of stuff to fill your mind, your presentations and your career.

Sitting and talking and kicking things around with bright and alert people can generate great stuff.

So much for thinking ... but we also need to be doing things

Learning how to behave better takes an effort too. The opportunities for surprising people with your actions are huge. We can dream but we also need to dazzle with our energy and decisiveness. Remember Harvard Business School. Remember the need for great execution.

Presenting your case

Learn how to do it and surprise yourself. If you can make yourself become a good presenter you will be in demand. Everyone loves an able presenter. So be shameless about how good you are and you'll start to surprise yourself at how talented you've become.

Being available to do presentations anywhere round the world is a brilliant way of making it and proving how valuable you are to your company.

Be nice in meetings and get results

Just learn how to be a genial presence who wants to get things done. Geniality is a much undervalued asset: it puts people at ease. It makes it easier to get decisions made. Nice really is OK. And why has no-one ever said before that being a good guy is an acceptable way of behaving? In fact the only acceptable way of behaving. (Nice by the way does not equal soft. It equals caring, considerate and tough.)

Make things happen

It's all very well to talk about action. You have to do it too. Most popular and successful people that I know are great project managers – people who really make things happen. Grab hold of things that need doing and do them. Prove that you are a 'doer'.

great project managers – people who really make things happen

An example of this was a very smart young woman I hired who transformed an organisation by literally going back to basics and stabilising it. Out of this came growth. She was a doer as well as a thinker but it was the doing that had the impact.

it was the doing that had the impact

Introduce new stuff to those around you

The ability to spot and enthuse about new developments in any market sector, or just in life in general, will mark you out from your more prosaic peers. It's always seemed to me that being an innovation talent scout makes you a more attractive human being. Because it makes you fun and alive and interesting. Surrounding yourself with new things seems to spark off new ideas and make more new things happen.

Help your colleagues and help yourself

This goes back to a simple 'team concept' theme. Be the person who goes out of their way to be useful and helpful to their peers. When you offer to help them, things that need doing get done.

It was an advertising person in the USA called Jerry Della Femina who created the meeting concept that at any given moment someone in his team was 'on duty and owning that meeting'. This is a great example of helping each other out and of 'teamwork'.

Work things out thoroughly

Don't just take things for granted, try to work them out properly. I was doing some work with a guy who runs a wealth company in Switzerland and we arrived at a very simple moral: 'If it seems too good to be true then it isn't true.' This very simple truth transformed part of his presentation and was a helpful stepping stone in an argument.

Learn to write clearly and simply

So few people seem to be able to write clearly nowadays that it's really worth putting in the hours trying to become a competent writer. People who can put together a well-crafted report are very employable and easy to promote. People who can be persuasive on the page earn a fortune at the top of their trade in advertising. Writing simply, well and with conviction is a winning skill.

Applaud change

The accepted wisdom from all the management gurus is that change is brilliant. General Eric Shinseki, the US Army General who correctly predicted a lot about the Iraq war, said: 'If you don't like change, you're going to like irrelevance even less.' Whilst the irrepressible Tom Peters goes even further. Try this:

We are on the verge of the biggest and most profound wave of economic change in a thousand years ... We avoid failure at all costs, and cling to ideals like 'order' and 'efficiency'. But we must embrace failure; we must glory in the very murk and muck and mess that yield true innovation.

Hmm, I think the message is that change is here to stay. Don't hide from it.

But I think – more to the point – that doers are going to be better if they understand they are playing in a fast-moving ball game where their actions may have to change quite radically in the light of new dynamics.

Re-launch yourself ... see how it changes your energy

And as part of the 'change crusade' of actions that transform your chances, start with yourself. Take a long hard look at yourself and come up with a manageable list of things that will change the way you are perceived by your bosses and peers. Perhaps more important than that, the effect on yourself of a makeover will be to refresh the way you yourself behave.

Be creative, think laterally, be surprising

Creativity is the ability to make connections between things which haven't been made before, it's about seeing patterns, it's about creating energy and it's about finding unusual solutions. What creativity does is dazzle and surprise.

what creativity does is dazzle and surprise

It's a big subject and another book. Creativity is certainly magical and the ability to see how to solve problems differently will be the biggest career differentiator in the future. If you get a chance to go on a creativity course take it and see what happens to you.

The whole idea of being a person with many strings to your bow is to place yourself right in the centre of the 21st-century stage. Be the person who gets things done and who can think their way out of a difficult situation.

Never before in most people's lifetimes have we needed flexibility and versatility so much. We must (all of us) learn to 'thrive on chaos' (the title of a brilliant book by Tom Peters).

Things to think about

◆ *This is the world of magic and juggling.*

◆ *Welcome to it.*

◆ *The ability to think and do and be magically creative is going to be at the very core of the successful careerist and the successful company in the future.*

◆ *Think James Dyson meets Warren Buffett meets Steve Jobs meets Steven Spielberg meets Lee Westwood.*

◆ *I am not just talking about the ability to paint, draw, sing or write poetry. I am talking about the ability to think differently and with a totally fresh competitive focus.*

Conclusion

A master class in accelerating your career

This is a hypothetical masterclass debating the top tips. See what works best for you and join in the discussion.

YES, I CAN SEE LOTS OF HANDS GOING UP and, yes, it's right that this isn't a one-size-fits-all world and that different things will work better for different people. Like you, sir, yes you in the third row with the greasy hair and the corduroy – is it corduroy, it's rather hard to tell? – and the grey ... sorry, the white shirt – you found the chapter on **'the power to attract'** most valuable? Hmm! I'd read it again, sir, and take it to heart. You may recall we called this the 'don't let yourself down chapter'.

And you Sophie, you found the chapter on **learning** resonated with you. Why was that? The increasing presence of mini-business schools in the big firms and that quaint rhyme someone in HR coined 'the more you learn, the more you earn'. But you also love learning don't you, so this introduces a whole new component of enjoyment to the work you do.

And I guess I know what you thought was the most important thing for you, Gregory – I've never seen anyone with so much energy in my life. Stop laughing for a moment and tell me. No, I very much doubt if you do want to be a Black Hole. So why does **the enthusiasm concept** grab you so strongly? Enthusiasm is infectious. In a world where carrying people with you is vital it's the easiest vehicle to fuel. Not for everyone I guess but I agree that it makes the world a better place and do not contemplate putting anyone near sales and marketing who isn't brimming over with it.

> *So why does the enthusiasm concept grab you so strongly?*

Anyone else? Yes you, sir, at the back. Sorry, can you speak up? You are a cynic? No, surely not. You believe 100% of effort needs to be spent on squaring off your boss? That you can only get anywhere in your career if **your boss** is on side. That goes too far, surely. What about your boss's boss – let's assume he's no fool? He can probably spot what's going on very clearly. OK, I get it, you exaggerated first off to get my attention. You're saying if you had to treat this as a game of roulette, your boss would be the most important number.

Ben? You think **the team thing** sucks. OK Ben, don't hold back, say what you really think. Yes there's been a lot about the power of the great leader but don't you think increasingly it's the team that makes the difference? You don't? Anyone disagree? Diana … Well that was an eloquent tribute to Arsenal Football Club and how they can lose their best players and become a better team. You believe the power of the team united on a common mission is hard to resist – that's, for instance, what made Avon so great a sales team or makes John Lewis so compelling a shopping experience – ask the chairman and he'll say it's the teamwork of their partners that accounts for their amazing success. I agree with you that, as a career driver, evidence of being a great team player really matters. I also think current management thinking is too focused on talent and leadership and far too little focused on team development.

Mary? Why is the Irish question relevant? Oh, I get it 'if I was going to Dublin I wouldn't start from here'. So you think this is about fixing a destination and single-mindedly **setting an achievable route map** to get there. Yes, it is logical. Yes, it is what you'd do if you were running a business. And how many of you think this strategic approach is the key thing to go for? Interesting, about a quarter. Yes, Tom … have I noticed anything about the quarter who just put their hands up? They're the ones most likely to go into banking, accountancy or consultancy and (frighteningly) the ones most likely to earn top whack. An interesting observation that, Tom. What about you?

Listening – that lost art. Why? Because you think it links into both learning and responsiveness and that if you become a great listener you get to learn and you learn to respond. OK so choose listening and you get two free. Yes, go on. You think that most of what goes wrong today is related to poor communication and that poor communication is almost exclusively to do with poor listening skills. And you'd even go so far as to make all modern executives go on listening courses.

*logic and strategy fly
out of the window*

Sonia? For you the ability to get a really good fix on who, what and where you are, is the key. Right, but why? Because you believe that just as we don't do easy stuff like listen properly so we take the most obvious stuff like **our own skills and capacity** for granted. When it comes to ourselves we are totally intuitive; logic and strategy fly out of the window. Very good. You feel quite strongly about this? Good analogy. If we were a gun we'd spend our time going 'ready, fire, aim and hope for the best'.

Anyone else? Yes. Sorry, I've forgotten your name. Hermione ... surely not, I thought it was Jane? Oh, I see you want to be a magician as well as a thinker and a doer. What's all that about? A sense that the sort of life you want to lead and the sort of business you'd like to work in would rely on **new business models**. Like? OK, Body Shop, Innocent, Google, Apple, Hotel du Vin, Naked ... OK, I get it. And sorry, I missed that. If you were a bloke you'd be talking about total football and as it is you want to talk about total business – where everyone on the team has a roving role shadowing everyone else. Where the most important words are 'new' and 'now' and 'never done like this before'. How many of you agree with this creative vision? Only a few. I think if you've got it flaunt it Hermione/Jane. Go for it and good luck.

Martin? You think they are all wrong. Hmmm, good positive start, Martin, go on. We live in a marketplace where the only differentiator is **our ability to respond better and faster**. This is a 'who jumps first and furthest argument' but what if you are being asked to reduce quality; how would this square with running a great as opposed to a fast-food restaurant? OK so it's responding in context and making sure 'the-customer-who's-always-right' feels he's being treated properly. And it's entirely about how you control time in a response situation. Oh, I quite like that 'as the supplier make sure it's you with your finger on the rewind or the fast forward button'. Anyone agree with Martin? A lot of almost yeses there. What? Well, yes I suppose saying being great at responding to requests might sound a slightly subservient way of climbing the career ladder but be realistic, we are talking about how to do well not how to behave as CEO.

Sorry, Louise? You think the mindset which is expressed in 'walking on water' does it most for you. Go on. The difference between being as good as you could be and as poor as you wish you weren't is a wide one created by how you feel about '**Brand Me**'. All the stuff here helps – every aspect creates say 10% of the engine, a brilliant career engine. But there's one thing missing. Which is … fuel. It's the WOW factor that will transform this engine from a work of potential power into a noisy, active thing. Thanks, that's helpful.

Let's draw things to a close here.

Winning at work will happen to you if you understand yourself better; decide what you want; use your capacity to learn; listen to what's going on; be happy in your work and positive in your outlook; help your boss have a better life; be part of a great team – in fact, be team coach; be attractive – fun to be with and in control of yourself; be a new age worker – where anything is possible in your life; and be a brilliant response machine.

Now class, is that too much to ask?

Do those as well as you can and the WOW feeling will follow. One final thing from me, because I'm an enthusiast, and that's this:

Enjoy your work even when that's hard and don't leave things undone that you ought to do. Just be very active, very positive, very focused and go for it.

Oh, and remember, be careful out there.

Postscript 2010

This book was originally written in 2007 and published the following year.

When I was writing it, all was well on the global economic front (apparently) and penniless Mexican gardeners who were being persuaded to buy Californian mansions seemed happy with their lot as did the guys who'd arranged their mortgages.

Then the wheels came off the global economy.

The whole idea of succeeding at work became a lot more challenging and the bigger issue was whether you had a job and therefore work at which you could succeed.

People spoke wistfully of the return to normal when it was clear that there was no stable definition of normal and that the world had changed forever.

But the lessons in the book remain valid and in revising it I've kept an eye on the context in which success actually can be achieved now. The key demand is going to be how fast-footed people can be.

Imagine the next decade as one in which any of the following may happen.

- There's pressure on margins.
- Markets decline.
- Competition hots up.
- Credit dries up (again).
- Overall activity slows down.

What will be required is an ability to revise strategy and business plans very fast; a need for willing adaptability and a maximisation of energy.

But the real secret will be in marketing and selling, intensifying efforts to promote your brands and yourself.

It will be innovation, branding and the ability to add value that will mark the winners from the losers. And all of these activities lie at the very heart of marketing.

From 2010 onwards success at work will be with those who can persuade people to buy what they have to sell.

And, one other thing, we're all going to have to work harder (not at the expense of our health though – take plenty of quality time off to recharge your batteries).

Suddenly business has become an 'extreme sport'.

Good luck – after all it could be worse.

RMH 18 May 2010
richard@hallogram.freeserve.co.uk
www.richardhall.biz
http://marketing-creativity-leadership.blogspot.com

Recent books:
Brilliant Presentation
Brilliant Marketing
Brilliant Business Creativity

The secrets of success in
coaching
10 ways to excel
as a coach

Mick Cope

9780273731849

The secrets of success in
marketing
20 ways to accelerate
your marketing
performance

Ian Linton

9780273742449

The secrets of success in
selling
12 ways to achieve
exceptional results

Nicola Cook

9780273730095

The secrets of success in
management
20 ways to survive
and thrive

Andrew Leigh

9780273720348

Unlock the secrets of
success

The *Secrets of Success* series contains all the insider knowledge and pearls of wisdom that the very best in the business already know and that you need to get ahead. In just a few simple steps they can be yours too.

They'll motivate you, inspire you and propel you from ordinary to extraordinary. Make today your first day as an expert; take action, learn from the best and discover the *Secrets of Success*.

☆ Everything you need to know to be the best you can be.

☆ Busts the myths, demystifies the jargon and reveals the real truths.

☆ Straightforward, easy to follow and enjoyable to read.

☆ Covering core business skills and subjects, each with a proven sales history.

www.pearson-books.com